DATE DUE   16564

Religion in Colonial America

Religion in American Life

JON BUTLER & HARRY S. STOUT
GENERAL EDITORS

Religion in Colonial America

Jon Butler

OXFORD UNIVERSITY PRESS
New York • Oxford

To the memory of three wonderful teachers and friends:
Anita Rutman, Darrett Rutman, and Paul Lucas

Oxford University Press

Oxford   New York
Athens Auckland Bangkok Bogotá Buenos Aires Calcutta
Cape Town   Chennai   Dar es Salaam   Delhi   Florence   Hong Kong   Istanbul
Karachi Kuala Lumpur Madrid Melbourne Mexico City Mumbai
Nairobi Paris São Paulo Singapore Taipei Tokyo Toronto Warsaw
and associated companies in
Berlin   Ibadan

Copyright © 2000 by Jon Butler

Published by Oxford University Press, Inc.
198 Madison Avenue, New York, New York 10016
www.oup.com

Oxford is a registered trademark of Oxford University Press

Library of Congress Cataloging-in-Publication Data

Butler, Jon. 1940–
Religion in Colonial America/Jon Butler.
p. cm. — (Religion in American life)
Includes index.
Summary: Presents the role of religion in early American life as well as the
influence of various groups on American religion during the Colonial era.
ISBN 0-19-511998-3 (alk. Paper)
United States—Religion—To 1800—Juvenile literature.
[1. United States—Religion—To 1800. 2. Religion.] I. Title. II. Series.
BL2525.B89 1999   200'.973'0903—dc21   99-046294

ISBN 0-19-511998-3 (library edition)

9 8 7 6 5 4 3 2 1

Printed in the United States of America
on acid-free paper

Design and layout: Loraine Machlin
Picture research: Patricia Burns

On the cover: "Wesley Chapel on John Street" by Joseph Beekman Smith.
Frontispiece: A wedding party approaches Boston's Old South Church in this 1756 tapestry.

Contents

Editors' Introduction

JON BUTLER & HARRY S. STOUT, GENERAL EDITORS

Colonial America has always seemed an especially religious place, an impression reinforced by images of Puritans entertaining American Indians at Thanksgiving or of demure Quakers settling peacefully in Pennsylvania. In fact, the religious vitality of early America stretched far beyond the typical stories of Puritans and Quakers. By the 1730s, colonial America teemed with an abundance of European religious groups. American Indians and Africans practiced and transformed their traditional religious systems. Philadelphia emerged as a capital of American Protestantism, and new church buildings and new religious practices, including revivals, utterly transformed the pre-Revolutionary spiritual landscape.

Religion in Colonial America captures the tumultuous, unexpected evolution of religion in Britain's American colonies. During the colonial period native and immigrant Americans dramatically altered the interaction between religion and daily life, and prepared the way for the startling passage of the First Amendment that ended national support for religious organizations and guaranteed freedom of worship. *Religion in Colonial America* stresses the multiplicity of religious expression in early America, the rise and fall of plans for religious orthodoxy and perfection, the roles of women, the spiritual ingenuity and perseverance of American Indians and Africans, the relationship between religion and government, and the

Late 17th-century wealth and artisan skills made it possible for colonists to construct large, refined church buildings such as the Old Ship Meeting House in Hingham, Massachusetts, built in 1681.

fateful connections among religion, the American Revolution, and the shaping of the new republic.

This book is part of a unique 17-volume series that explores the evolution, character, and dynamics of religion in American life from 1500 to the end of the 20th century. As late as the 1960s, historians paid relatively little attention to religion beyond studies of New England's Puritans. But since then, American religious history and its contemporary expression have been the subject of intense inquiry. These new studies have thoroughly transformed our knowledge of almost every American religious group and have fully revised our understanding of religion's role in U.S. history.

It is impossible to capture the flavor and character of the American experience without understanding the connections between secular activities and religion. Spirituality stood at the center of Native American societies before European colonization and has continued to do so long after. Religion—and the freedom to express it—motivated millions of immigrants to come to the United States from remarkably different cultures, and the exposure to new ideas and ways of living shaped their experience. It also fueled tension among different ethnic and racial groups in America and, regretfully, accounted for difficult episodes of bigotry in American society. Religion urged Americans to expand the nation—first within the continental United States, then through overseas conquests and missionary work—and has had a profound influence on American politics, from the era of the Puritans to the present. Finally, religion contributes to the extraordinary diversity that has, for four centuries, made the United States one of the world's most dynamic societies.

The Religion in American Life series explores the historical traditions that have made religious freedom and spiritual exploration central features of American society. It emphasizes the experience of religion in America—what men and women have understood by religion, how it has affected politics and society, and how Americans have used it to shape their daily lives.

Religion in American Life

JON BUTLER & HARRY S. STOUT
GENERAL EDITORS

יהוה

IHS

LE GRAND
VOYAGE DV PAYS
des Hurons, situé en L'A:
merique uers la mer douce
ez dernieres confins de
la nouuelle France

Ou il est traicté de tout
ce qui est du pays & du
gouuernement des Sauuages

Auec un Dictionnaire
de la Langue huronne

Par Fr. Gabriel Sagard
Recollect de St François
de la prouince St Denis

Jaspar Isac f

S. F.

B. F. M. D. V.

A. PARIS Chez Denys
Moreau rue St Jacques à
La Salamandre 1632

CABANE

Chapter 1

Worlds Old and New

The French Jesuit Pierre de Charlevoix was fascinated by the religious customs of the Algonquian-speaking Indians of southern Canada and northern New York and New England. In his two-volume *Journal of a Voyage to North-America* (1761), Charlevoix related many stories about Algonquian religion that seemed both wonderful and strange. Charlevoix was especially intrigued by Algonquian dreaming and its dramatic effect among traditional Algonquian believers. He was particularly taken by a story told to him by French Jesuit missionaries working among the Algonquian Indians. An Algonquian man dreamed that he had been a prisoner held by Algonquian enemies. When he awoke, he was confused and afraid. What did the dream mean? When he consulted the Algonquian shaman, the figure who mediated between humans, the gods, and nature, the shaman told him he had to act out the implications of the dream. The man had himself tied to a post, and other Algonquians burned several parts of his body, just as would have happened had his captivity been real.

For Algonquian-speaking Indians and other eastern woodlands Indians, dreams and visions gave signals about life that must be followed. The dreams and visions exposed dangers, revealed opportunities, and explained important principles. Dreams demonstrated that the souls of men and women existed separately from the body. The souls of others spoke to the living through dreams, including the souls of the dead.

When Algonquians dreamed about elk, they felt encouraged because the elk was a symbol of life. But when Algonquians dreamed about bears, they became afraid because the bear signified the approach of death.

The Algonquian dream episodes signaled the compelling interrelationship between the Indians' religious life and their day-to-day existence. Dreams and visions allowed spirits to communicate with Indians who revealed eternal values. Dreams and visions evoked ordinary emotions and everyday circumstances to explain how the world worked. They described where each individual fit in a universe that otherwise seemed so often disconcerting and confusing. For Indians, dreams revealed how thoroughly religion was not merely "belief," but an intimate and interactive relationship among humans, the supernatural, and nature. As Charlevoix put it, "in whatever manner the dream is conceived, it is always looked upon as a thing sacred, and as the most ordinary way in which the gods make known their will to men."

Judith Giton did not want to go to America. She was a French Protestant, or "Huguenot," in the village of La Voulte in Languedoc in southern France. But in 1682 the French king, Louis XIV, began using soldiers to enforce restrictions on Protestant worship in La Voulte, sometimes with violence. As Judith Giton wrote years later in a memoir, the village "suffered through eight months [of] exactions and quartering…by the soldiery, with much evil." With her mother and two brothers, Pierre and Louis, she decided "to go out of France by night, and leave the soldiers in bed." The Gitons fled to Lyon and Dijon, then on to Cologne, Germany, where they met other refugee Huguenots. Judith, Louis, and their mother fervently believed they should settle 30 miles from Cologne with another brother. But Pierre had read a pamphlet advertising a colony in America—South Carolina, a place with many opportunities as well as freedom of religion. Pierre had "nothing but Carolina on his thoughts," Judith wrote.

Pierre won the argument. He took Judith, Louis, and their mother to Amsterdam and then London to book passage for South Carolina. The voyage to the New World turned out to be a disaster. Mother Giton died of scarlet fever. Their ship's captain left the three Giton children in Bermuda, where they had to find another ship for South Carolina. Louis

died of a fever 18 months after arriving in South Carolina. Although Judith and Pierre survived, she remembered the ordeal as extremely difficult. She experienced much "sickness, pestilence, famine, poverty [and] very hard work. I was in this country a full six months without tasting bread." Later she married another Huguenot refugee in South Carolina, Pierre Manigault. "God has had pity on me, and has changed my lot to one more happy," she wrote. "Glory be unto him."

Sometime in late 1723, the Protestant bishop of London, who had informal responsibility for Church of England affairs in America, received a wrenching petition from slaves in Virginia. It was unsigned, written by a mulatto slave "baptized and brought up in the way of the Christian faith." He described how the masters were harsh with him and all other slaves, "as hard with us as the Egyptians was with the children of Israel….To be plain, they do look no more upon us than if we were dogs." Masters kept

Louis XIV abolished the limited Protestant worship permitted in France in the 1680s and persecuted and tortured Huguenots, including even high-ranking French men and women.

Africans enslaved in Virginia petitioned the Anglican bishop of London for freedom in 1723. They charged that slaveholders "do look no more upon us than if we were dogs" and kept Africans "in ignorance of our salvation."

the slaves "in ignorance of our salvation… kept out of the church, and matrimony is denied [to] us." The slaves begged the bishop for opportunities to learn "the Lord's Prayer, the creed, and the Ten Commandments." They hoped that their children could "be put to school and learned to read through the Bible."

The Africans feared for their lives in writing this petition. If their masters were to discover the document "we should go near to swing upon the gallows' tree." But they wrote anyway. They hoped that the bishop, "Lord King George, and the rest of the rulers will release us out of this cruel bondage, and this we beg for Jesus Christ's his sake, who has commanded us to seek first the kingdom of God and all things shall be added unto us."

These slaves need not have worried about the effects of their petition. It was ignored in London and remained unknown in Virginia despite many rumors about slave dissatisfaction and rebellions in that colony throughout the 1720s. After being received in London, the petition was misfiled with papers on Jamaica; it was discovered by historians only in the 1990s, its author unknown now as then. And the petition's eloquent pleas remained unfulfilled, in Virginia as in the other British colonies. Through most of the colonial period, religion never disturbed the advance of slavery.

Nathan Cole had been bothered by religious questions for some time. Twenty-nine years old, a carpenter and a farmer, Cole lived in Kensington, Connecticut. In 1739 he heard that the British revivalist George Whitefield had arrived in the colonies. When Cole wrote many years later about his experience hearing Whitefield, he remembered the event vividly.

Now it pleased God to send Mr. Whitefield into this land....I longed to see and hear him, and wished he would come this way. I heard he was come to New York and the Jerseys and great multitudes flocking after him...next I heard he was at Long Island, then at Boston....Then of a sudden, in the morning about 8 or 9 of the clock there came a messenger and said Mr. Whitefield preached at Hartford and Wethersfield yesterday and is to preach at Middletown this morning at ten of the clock. I was in my field at work, I dropped my tool that I had in my hand and ran home to my wife telling her to make ready quickly to go and hear Mr. Whitefield.

On high land I saw before me a cloud or fog raising. I first thought it came from the great [Connecticut] river, but as I came nearer the road, I heard a noise something like a low rumbling thunder....It was the noise of horses feet coming down the road and this cloud was a cloud of dust made by the horses feet....When we got to Middletown['s] old meeting house there was a great multitude, it was said to be 3000 or 4000 people assembled together.... The land and banks over the river looked black with people and horses....I saw no man at work in his field, but all seemed to be gone.

When I saw Mr. Whitefield come upon the scaffold he looked almost angelical; a young, slim, slender, youth before some thousands of people.... He looked as if he was clothed with the authority from the Great God...and my hearing him preach gave me a heart wound. By God's blessing, my old foundation was broken up, and I saw that my righteousness would not save me...all that I could do would not save me.

Within a year, Nathan Cole had undergone a "born again" experience, feeling guilt because of his sins but placing all his faith in God's forgiveness. He later joined an evangelical congregation that limited its membership to men and women who had had similar experiences, then left that congregation to join an evangelical Baptist church that limited the rite of baptism to believing or converted adults. Cole belonged to that congregation for another 40 years until he died in 1783 at the age of 72. How thoroughly religion affected individuals and society in early America can be difficult to understand. We have been taught to believe that our ancestors, especially our colonial ancestors, were remarkably pious, and indeed many were. Yet religion's importance for individuals and societies also produced numerous differences and antagonisms that leave a confusing picture of early American religion. In Europe, Catholics and Protestants opposed each other and then divided among themselves as a consequence of the Protestant Reformation that began in the 1520s, 30 years after Columbus's discovery of the Americas. National rivalries separated French Catholics from Spanish Catholics and Protestants in England from those in the Netherlands. In turn, theological differences caused many internal divisions among Catholics and Protestants. In Africa, language and cultural differences reinforced religious disagreements between different societies, while within the same society individuals often disagreed about the expression and practice of religion. The importance of nature in American Indian religions never guaranteed that all native groups would honor nature in similar ways; the contrasts in their religious customs produced discord between individuals and rivalries between societies.

As a result, religious expression was complicated throughout America. In Catholic France and Protestant England, among the Ibo and Ashanti peoples of Africa, and amid the Micmacs and Catawbas of America, religious expression emerged in many different ways. What and how these men and women thought about religion was important to them as individuals and to their societies. In crucial ways, their religious beliefs and practices often accounted for the distinctiveness of their societies. These differences and similarities—individual and national, linguistic and theological—became the foundation of the diverse, historically evolving experiences of religion that characterized the entire American experience, both before and after the American Revolution.

What did religion mean to men and women on the eve of European colonization in America? Many things, it turns out. When the British writer Henry Fielding published his comic novel *Tom Jones* in 1749, the Reverend Mr. Thwackum, Fielding's ludicrous Church of England, or Anglican, clergyman, became one of Fielding's most memorable characters. Thwackum's fussy description of "religion" exemplified the narrow-mindedness of Britain's mid-18th-century Anglican establishment that Fielding detested: "When I mention religion, I mean the Christian religion; and not only the Christian religion but the Protestant religion; and not only the Protestant religion, but the Church of England."

Unfortunately for Thwackum, reality was—and long would be—far more complex in Britain and throughout Europe, Africa, and America. In

Europe, state-supported churches formally monopolized public worship and gave each nation an appearance of unanimity in religion. Clearly, politics played a major role in determining both national and local religious commitments, as symbolized in the phrase "whose Prince, whose Church." Because King Henry VIII willed it, England became Protestant, and all English men and women legally became members of the Church of England once it had separated from the Roman Catholic Church. But then England switched back to Catholicism under Mary I, after which Elizabeth I brought the nation back to Protestantism. France and Spain remained Catholic because their monarchs remained Catholics. The numerous German principalities presented a patchwork of faiths. Most of the northern princes, including the king of Prussia, chose Protestantism, whereas many of their southern counterparts, including the rulers of Saxony, chose Catholicism.

In England, the royal command that created the Church of England fanned further religious debate. Elizabeth I controlled demands for wider reform of the Church of England better than any of her successors did. She eliminated practices that seemed Catholic yet vigorously suppressed radical Protestants. In the 1580s she simply forbade meetings by Protestant "schismatics" who sought to split off from the official church, the Church of England, and enforced her orders with remarkable success.

Elizabeth's successor, King James I, who had previously been King James VI of Scotland, experienced greater frustration in matters of religion. By his reign reformers were demanding more changes in the Church of England. As their numbers multiplied under James, opponents

Seventeenth-century men and women often ridiculed effete and fussy clergymen. This cartoon compared clergymen in politics to monkeys in toy shops: Both "may do much Mischief, but cannot possibly do any Good."

decried them as "Puritans"—rigorous, overly demanding religious zealots. By the time King James asked the Archbishop of Canterbury, William Laud, to suppress the Puritans in the 1620s, they were too numerous to put down easily. The effort, often poorly planned and clumsily executed, initiated debates in the 1630s that ultimately produced major parliamentary confrontations, the English Civil War of the 1640s, and the beheading of James's son, Charles I, in 1649.

As a result, by the 1690s England possessed a seemingly endless array of religious groups, which helps explain Thwackum's prissy bitterness about the meaning of the term *religion*. Most English men and women formally remained Anglicans, or members of the Church of England. But many others were Congregationalists, Presbyterians, Baptists, and Quakers—all Protestants, as were the Anglicans—and some even remained Catholics despite the century-long attack on their church and the social and political penalties that English Catholics endured. In addition, England also contained a small number of Jews, concentrated mostly in London and the port towns, not unlike the urban pattern of Jewish residence throughout the European continent. The 1689 Toleration Act grudgingly recognized this diversity. Although the act did not legitimize Catholics or Jews and required officeholders to be Anglicans, it permitted at least some dissenting Protestants to worship, including Congregationalists, Presbyterians, and Quakers, and thus marked an important step toward modern religious freedom.

Important as religious identity was, however, actual participation in public worship in fact varied greatly, not only in England but throughout Europe. In England, for example, religion sometimes seemed only the indulgence of "enthusiasts." While Puritan reformers or Quakers pursued religious truth and the most adamant Anglicans sought to suppress them, many English men and women seldom participated in worship. A minister in Hertfordshire, England, complained in 1572 that on Sunday "a man may find the churches empty, saving the minister and two or four lame, and old folke; for the rest are gone to follow the Devil's daunce." This apathy was not confined to England. In the 1590s in Toulouse, France, only 2 to 5 percent of the laity (as opposed to priests and nuns) attended weekly mass, even though more than 90 percent of adults took Easter communion. A 1584 census of Antwerp, Belgium, revealed both significant religious diversity and considerable apathy: About 9 percent of household heads said they were Lutheran, 21 percent said they were Calvinist, some 30 percent claimed to be Catholic, and about 40 percent failed to specify any religious affiliation.

Individual beliefs also varied. Although open atheism was uncommon, a surprising number of people expressed not only criticism of specific groups but also doubt about religion altogether. Doing so proved to be dangerous. As late as 1697, a Scottish boy was hanged for denying the truth of the Bible. Some men and women denied the existence of God, of heaven and hell, and of heavenly rewards for good behavior. At least one woman believed in the Devil but not in God: "She thinks the Devil doth tempt her to do evil to herself and she doubteth whether there is a God." A man in Yorkshire called preaching "bibble babble" and said that he would "rather hear a cuckoo sing."

Many Europeans believed in magic. Magic invoked the supernatural without any necessary reference to God or Christianity, and Europeans everywhere knew thousands of magical practitioners. Some were learned scholars, including John Dee, whom Queen Elizabeth hired to cast horoscopes—astrological forecasts based on the alignment of the planets and stars—and William Lilly, who told fortunes and cast horoscopes for more than 4,000 well-paying London clients in the 1640s and 1650s.

"Wise men" and "wise women," usually illiterate, practiced cruder forms of magic for the common people. One official in Lincolnshire described them as using books that contained occult or magical information, "old mouldy almanacks, and several sheets of astrological schemes, all drawn false and wrong." Nevertheless, they attracted men and women who wished to know the future, find lost or stolen objects, know good days on which to conceive children, or who hoped for cures from diseases of themselves, their children and relatives, or of valuable animals they owned.

Europeans sometimes mixed magic and Christianity—to the dismay of the Christian clergy. One 17th-century skeleton recovered in a modern archaeological excavation bore a neck charm with the inscription "Jesus

An angry client seeks revenge for false predictions drawn from salamanders (said to possess secret knowledge), planetary configurations, and animal parts. Astrologers, alchemists, and occultists all practiced their arts in colonial America.

Christ for mercy sake, take away this toothache." One Anglican minister recorded in his diary how he mixed the two himself when, in desperation, he gave an insane women an amulet with "some verses of John I written in a paper to hang about her neck, as also certayn herbes to drive the Devil out of her."

Amid this variety and confusion, traditional institutional religion—Catholicism, Protestantism, and Judaism, especially—provided reassurance to believers and important formal religious structures for society. Above all, traditional institutional religion dominated the visual landscape. The European countryside, towns, and cities teemed with religious buildings, ranging from small chapels to immense cathedrals and, in the Jewish ghettos of cities and towns, synagogues. Many 16th- and 17th-century church authorities complained that the buildings outnumbered their priests, ministers, and rabbis and that they could not staff all the possible pulpits.

Public Christian worship also commanded more sustained and cohesive loyalty from laypeople than did private practices, including magic, despite complaints by clergymen about the influence of magic and popular religious indifference. Throughout Europe, large numbers of men and women served the state-supported churches. In Catholic countries, priests, monks, and nuns often accounted for as much as 10 to 15 percent of the adult population. Even though Protestants abolished monasteries, an enormous number of clergymen were needed to serve Protestant interests. As European colonization began in America, thousands of Protestant clergymen were working throughout Europe, from Germany to England and Scotland. Because most of them served the churches supported by their governments, their influence extended far beyond their individual endeavors.

Above all, institutional religion explained how and why the world was the way it was and told believers what they could expect in this life and the next. Catholics found both order and relevance in the authority of the pope, in the timeless truth of the seven sacraments (especially the Mass, in which wine and bread became Christ's blood and body that had been sacrificed so that all believers could live forever), and in the panoply of the saints whose shrines dotted Europe and whose miraculous healing of the sick and injured testified to Christianity's truth and power.

Protestants celebrated the sovereignty of God and God's exclusive grant of salvation, which could not be earned with money or human labor. They believed they had reconstructed the worship and theology of the early church, and placed great stress on the sermon that replaced the ritual of the Catholic Mass as the central feature of worship. Whereas Catholics stressed miracles in the cure of disease and injury, Protestants stressed prayer, although some Protestants, such as the Englishman George Fox, the founder of Quakerism, performed miracles to demonstrate the truth of his new religion.

Jews honored God's commandments set out in the Torah for God's chosen people. These beliefs, duties, and rituals were further elucidated by centuries of Talmudic scholarship, the ancient Jewish rabbinical writings, that explicated biblical commandments for modern men and women. The study of the Talmudic writings, developing Jewish theology, and interchanges among different Jewish communities and with Christians shaped Jewish life across Europe from Russia to Spain in a continuing diaspora now almost 1,500 years old.

The New World provided fresh territory for Old World religious traditions. For Catholics and Protestants alike, the New World offered millions of "heathen" souls to be converted. Spanish and Portuguese Catholics saw the native peoples of South America and Mexico as God's challenge to Christian missions. They destroyed as many examples of native culture as they could (some Aztec and Inca buildings proved impossible to demolish) and imposed the Mass everywhere they could, thus giving the areas they conquered the new name of "Latin" America, because the Mass was observed in Latin.

England's James I chartered the Virginia Company to bring Christianity to Indians living "in darkness" and in "miserable ignorance of the true knowledge and worship of God." As a result, the New World presented new arenas for religious and national contests that had become all too familiar in the Old World. Who would win the souls of the New World's peoples, and who would conquer the territory they occupied?

For Jews, the New World represented something quite different: another place of exile in the face of persistent and renewed persecution. In 1492, the year Columbus discovered America, Queen Isabella ordered all Spanish Jews to leave the country or convert to Christianity, a climax to several centuries of Spanish Christian persecution of Jews. Some Jews fled the country; others (called Marranos, meaning Jews forcibly converted to Christianity) converted publicly but practiced Judaism secretly. Not surprisingly, throughout the colonial period some Jews also emigrated to America, hoping not merely for survival but for freedom as well, as would be true of many 17th- and 18th-century Christian emigrants to America.

Understanding African and American Indian religion before European colonization is difficult, because the literary sources that provide a broad profile of European religion are seldom available for precolonial African and American societies. Moreover, the archaeological evidence

usually is insufficient to portray the vast array of individual and group differences in religion within societies that were known to exist in America before 1800. Yet we know that religious expression in these societies was rich and complex. Anthropologists and historians have long demonstrated that the religions of preliterate societies were exceptionally sophisticated, easily rivaling Christianity, Judaism, Islam, and other major world religious systems.

Certainly, the Africans and Europeans of the colonial period shared beliefs in a finite earthly life and an infinite afterlife. They also believed that supernatural figures and forces shaped both lives. Jean Barbot, a European traveler in western Africa in the 1670s, argued that many Africans believed in a supreme being who determined when people were born and when they died, who caused events to happen, and who ruled

Leaders of the Spanish Inquisition of the late 16th century prosecuted heretics and alleged witches and forced Jews to convert to Catholicism or burn at the stake, although Jews had previously lived in Spain with considerable but not perfect freedom.

the afterlife. A Dutch traveler named William Bosman observed that Africans understood the "idea of the True God and ascribe to him the Attributes of Almighty, and Omnipresent," not unlike the Christians. At the same time, these Africans did not always offer sacrifices or even prayers to this god, because the god "is too high exalted above us, and too great to condescend so much as to trouble himself or think of Mankind."

West Africans believed in a great variety of spirits that determined what happened in this life and the next. Some believed that the "high god" or "creator of the world" constructed the lesser spirits or gods. Many of these gods had specialized characteristics. The Ga peoples of western Africa, for example, honored no "high god," and each Ga village was protected by a god senior to all other Ga deities. The Yoruba peoples honored Olorun as their high god and performed sacrifices in this deity's name to a panoply of minor gods. Gods of the rain, of thunder or lightning, and of the waterways shaped secular and human events. And like the spirits that inhabited or governed animals, they also sometimes competed with each other.

Africans fashioned remarkable varieties of religious expression. For example, many societies believed in and practiced augury or divination, the predicting of things to come. Religious leaders of considerable stature discerned revelations in the arrangements in plants or rocks and interpreted dreams and visions. In Mbundu society in the area of modern Angola, it was thought that events might be predicted by understanding the behavior of animals, the arrangement of leaves, bird calls, or the configuration of the stars. Although the process might have been similar to some forms of European magic, the specific details were unique to each society. In the Yoruba culture, in the area of modern Nigeria, a priest practicing Whydah threw cowry shells on a board and asked the spirits to make the shells land in such a way as to allow him to predict events.

Africans also believed in religious revelations communicated by supernatural beings to humans. These beings intervened in human events to teach people important religious lessons. Africans received religious revelations through spirit "mediums" who passed on messages from supernatural powers and gods. Indeed, revelations were everyday occurrences in many African societies. They were not relegated to ancient times, as in the Christian Old Testament and Jewish Torah. Many revelations predicted modern events. For example, the king of Allada in West Africa believed that his vision of a new white childlike god predicted the later arrival of Europeans.

Other Africans communicated with the souls of the dead, especially dead ancestors. For example, Africans visited a *ngombo*, a spirit medium, when they wanted to know what had made them sick and what would cure their diseases. They also frequently believed in spirit possession, in which an evil spirit possessed the body of a person or animal to make them sick. Spirit possessions afflicted humans as well as animals and demonstrated the power of the spirit or god to others, just as early Christians performed miracles to demonstrate the validity of their faith. Finally, late-17th-century European travelers reported the existence of occasional atheists and doubters who cast aside particular religious traditions or rejected religion in general and lent individual variety to the societies in which they lived.

African religions underwent substantial historical change in the centuries before American colonization. As in Europe, in Africa wars and peaceful emigrations produced substantial alterations in the religions and religious practices of the African peoples. Islam, long a powerful religious force in eastern Africa, extended its influence into the western part of the continent in the centuries before the European colonization of America and the growth of the slave trade. Mosques could be found in western Africa in the 17th century, and Christian travelers were sometimes stunned by the devotion of African Muslims. "Foolas and Mandingoes attend to the ceremonial duties of their religion with such strictness as well might cause Christians to blush," wrote one 17th-century traveler. The kingdoms of Ghana, Mali, and Songhay became principal centers of Muslim influence in north central Africa as European colonization developed in the New World.

Like Christianity, traditional African religions often included carved figures in their rituals, such as this Oshe Shango, or dance wand for the thunder god.

The faces of Portuguese merchants are carved above the face of the king on this 16th-century ornamental mask for the Benin leader. European trade influenced not only the African economy but its politics and culture as well.

Christians also began proselytizing in West Africa in the 16th century but with only limited success. Portuguese Catholics were among the most insistent missionaries. In the 1530s they converted the principal king of the Kongo, Nzinga Mbemba, and baptized him as Dom Affonso I. The Portuguese also won converts in the small "creole" or mixed societies of Europeans and Africans that developed on the West African coast in the 17th and 18th centuries as a consequence of the slave trade, although major success in Christian missions in Africa did not occur until the mid-19th century.

In all, then, African religions were as dynamic and shaped by human actions in different ways and different times as were European religions. The African religions evolved substantially in the 13th, 14th, and 15th centuries, even before the arrival of European missionaries, slave traders, and conquerors. African religious practices changed as European encounters with both Africa and America accelerated in the 1500s. The arrival of Christians only complicated the changes that had already been occurring in African religious beliefs for centuries, just as the Protestant Reformation brought out tensions that had long existed within European Catholicism for centuries before the Reformation.

America's Indians also proved to be deeply religious. It is not easy to untangle the preconquest religious life of America's native peoples from romantic myths and self-serving criticisms of missionaries and other European observers throughout the colonial period. Still, archaeological evidence, astute travel and descriptive narratives, and artifacts collected from the earliest days of European settlement create a dramatic and nuanced view of the religious practices and beliefs among American Indians on the eve of European contact, conquest, and colonization.

America's Indians had created breathtaking numbers of different cultures and religions by the late 16th century. Most U.S. historians now estimate that at least 500 independent cultures, and perhaps more, existed in the area of the modern United States on the eve of European contact, but it is impossible to count with complete accuracy. Indeed, the area of modern California alone probably contained more than 200 different linguistic and cultural groups. Yet these late-16th-century Indian groups exhibited striking similarities in their religious beliefs and practices despite their many differences in language, economy, and society.

Many Indian religious systems believed that the world was one whole: They did not separate life into the secular and the sacred. The Indians often believed that they shared the world with supernatural beings and forces who rewarded and punished them and whom they encountered directly and indirectly through nature. Thus, for them religion was not a separate entity in their lives, something to turn to in times of difficulty or joy, but a part of daily existence. As they moved through the forests and deserts they talked to spirits, performed rites to honor them, saw them in visions and dreams, felt their reprobation in bee stings or nettle scratches, or found themselves cut down by the competing gods of alien nations sent to kill and conquer. For the Native Americans religion connected with all of life, from the seemingly trivial to the most consequential.

The Indians' religion often centered on maintaining intimate relationships with nature. The various Indian tribes typically viewed nature as powerful, all encompassing, and sacred. For example, the Micmacs of modern-day Nova Scotia and eastern Canada developed a religious system in which the beaver stood at the center of their cosmos, not as a god but as a symbol of the deeply spiritual relationship between the Micmacs and nature. One European missionary described hunting, especially for beaver, as a "holy occupation" among the Micmacs. The rules for hunting required strict adherence to honor that people's special relationship to nature. As a result, beavers were to be hunted in particular ways, with certain rituals. When beavers were trapped, for example, their blood was to be drawn in a public ritual that expressed the

This Moorish plate, with distinct Islamic decorative motifs, commemorated Portuguese voyages and trade in western Africa, where Christianity and Islam both competed and sometimes mixed.

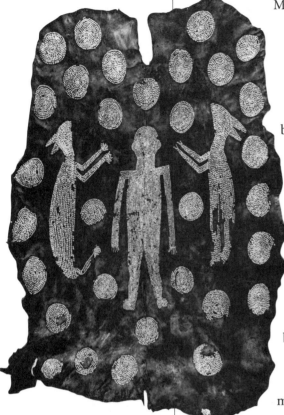

Powhatan, the Virginia Algonquian "king," supposedly owned this deerskin mantle decorated with shell beads. The 34 roundlets may represent villages controlled by Powhatan, and the white-tailed deer on the right and possible wolf or mountain lion on the left may represent sacred animals.

Micmacs' respect for the animal. Beaver bones could never be given to dogs, because the Micmacs believed that doing so would cause beavers to lose their sense of smell. And as one Frenchman observed, beaver bones never could be thrown away, "lest the spirit of the bones ... would promptly carry the news to the other beavers, which would desert the country in order to escape the same misfortune."

Shamans, who also acted as medicine men and women, interpreted the intimate relationship between humans and nature for the Native Americans. Shamans were individuals set aside by themselves or the community to serve as intermediaries among humans, nature, and the supernatural. Their societies' complex, difficult world needed the skills of sensitive, intelligent guides who understood the foibles of human beings as well as the mysterious ways of nature and the supernatural. In some Indian societies, such as the Mohawks, women served as shamans, in others only men served, and in still others both women and men served. Shamans often received guidance through dreams or visions. They demonstrated their status through cures that combined physical skill and training, such as setting broken bones, with prophetic and revelatory powers that provided the force behind secret medicines, prayers, and magical practices. Thus, American Indians, not unlike Africans as well as European Jews, Catholics, and Protestants, used religion not only to shape the way believers thought about the world but also to defend against injury and sickness brought on by both human and supernatural causes.

The religious concerns of Europeans, Africans, and Native Americans did indeed have certain elements in common; moreover, this was already apparent to some men and women of that time. One of these was William Moraley, a British emigrant who came to America in the 1720s. Moraley could not accept the Indians' rejection of the Christian God. Yet he had come to understand many, if not all, of the functions of Native American religions:

> As to their notions of Religion, they are very wild, having none establish'd among them; but believe there is a God, Creator of all Things, endowed with Wisdom, Goodness, and Mercy; and believe they shall be judged, punished, and rewarded, according as they observe the moral Precepts instilled into them by the Light of Nature, and the Tradition of their Fathers.

What Moraley understood about the American Indians could be fairly well applied to both Europeans and Africans at the time. What he did not understand well, however, was the dramatic change that was transforming religion among all those peoples even as he wrote. For Europeans, Africans, and Native Americans, the colonial period from 1580 to 1776 would witness major upheavals and transformations in the nature and expression of religion among all of them. European Catholics, Protestants, and Jews witnessed major growth and spread of their religious traditions in ways not even the most pious of them could have foreseen on the eve of the European settlement of America. Africans found many traditional religious beliefs and practices shattered by the ordeal of New World slavery. Yet they discovered crucial ways to sustain and practice both new and old religious convictions under the most difficult circumstances. American Indians suffered under immense difficulties as European-induced sickness and warfare destroyed whole societies and cultures. Their traditional ways of life were undermined by the work of Christian missionaries. Yet in the 18th century they emerged with new religious configurations that proved to be as crucial to their own future as had been the religious changes undergone by Europeans and Africans.

Throughout the era of European colonization, religious practices and beliefs in America were modified in response to changing circumstances. In turn, changing religious traditions altered the ways Europeans, Africans, and Native Americans experienced life. These powerful interactions made religion a major force everywhere in colonial American life.

THE PURITAN.

"To Banbury came I O profane one !
Where I saw a Puritane — one
Hanging of his cat on Monday
for killing of a Mouse on Sunday."

Vide Drunken Barnaby's Tour.

Chapter 2

Religion in the First Colonies

The English settlers of New England intended to make religion the focus of their settlement. These first immigrants were alienated English Puritans called separatists, who had already fled England for the Netherlands because of their inability to achieve further reformation in the Church of England at home. They originally received a charter for land in Virginia but landed instead near Plymouth, Massachusetts, in December 1620. They renegotiated their charter with London authorities and celebrated the famous first Thanksgiving with nearby Indians in October 1621.

A far larger body of settlers arrived in 1630 to establish a separate outpost, the Massachusetts Bay colony, north of the Plymouth colony. Facing continued persecution in England and led by the Cambridge-educated Puritan lawyer John Winthrop, these Puritans began to leave England in large numbers in 1630. By the end of 1630, 11 ships with more than 1,000 Puritan immigrants had landed in Salem, the first town established in the new colony. They then proceeded to establish a second town, Boston, named for Boston in England, a major Puritan center. By 1635 more than 5,000 additional Puritans had arrived in Massachusetts Bay.

John Winthrop, who soon became the governor of the Massachusetts Bay Company, described a powerful religiously centered vision for the new colony. Speaking aboard the *Arbella,* the flagship of the small Puritan

The Puritans emphasis on morals often brought them considerable criticism. One anti-Puritan verse criticized a Puritan for hanging his cat on Monday because it killed a "mouse on Sunday."

The Massachusetts governor John Winthrop led a colony whose residents, including church members, often failed to live up to his often inspiring religious and community idealism.

fleet, as it rested in Salem harbor before the settlers disembarked, Winthrop gave what would become one of the most renowned sermons in American history, a lay homily that he entitled "A Model of Christian Charity." These were not just alienated Puritans fleeing England, perhaps hoping to return, but men and women with a vision for the future in America. In his sermon Winthrop set down what he believed his followers should intend for this New World now that they had left England, that "sinful land."

Winthrop believed the Puritans should settle together in a city or town where large and small farmers and merchants alike would form a community housing their church, their government, and their defenses against enemies, whether Indian or European. He believed it would be a "city of God" and a "city upon a hill." The Puritans would worship as the Bible intended them to. Men and women would aid each other and, as a consequence, serve God. They would not satisfy individual desires at the expense of the community. "We must be knit together in this work as one man," Winthrop wrote. "We must entertain each other in brotherly affection.[W]e must delight in each other, make others' conditions our own, rejoice together, mourn together, labor and suffer together, always having before our eyes our commission and community in the work, our community as members of the same body."

The importance of religion in New England was not unique among England's American colonies. In 1619 the initial meeting of the first colonial legislative assembly, the Virginia House of Burgesses, took up religion as a major task. The Burgesses opened its first meeting with a prayer by the Rev. Richard Buck. "Men's affairs do little prosper where God's service is neglected," the Burgesses wrote. They then passed laws to uphold "God's service" in the New World wilderness. Ministers would preach every Sunday and all colonists would be required to attend. The laws banned idleness, drunkenness, gambling, and fancy dress. Reports of "all ungodly disorders," such as "dishonest company keeping with women and such like," would be presented by ministers and church wardens to

A Puritan Leader Speaks to Early American Emigrants

Before landing in Massachusetts in the spring of 1630, the English Puritan layman John Winthrop spoke to the assembled passengers on the ship Arbella, *explaining his view of what America could become. His thoughts, written in the essay, "A Model of Christian Charity," did not always guide the Massachusetts Bay Colony, even though he served as its governor for most of the years between his arrival in 1630 and his death in 1649. The settlers disagreed about religion, land, and politics in ways that distressed Winthrop. But his idealism remained a powerful beacon long after his death. His words have been invoked by Americans, including many presidents, again and again because they seem to capture the elusive meaning of community, even if later readers and listeners followed Winthrop's injunctions no better than the Puritans.*

Now the only way to avoid [a] shipwreck and to provide for our posterity is to follow the counsel of [the prophet] Micah, to doe justly, to love mercy, to walk humbly with our God. For this end, we must be knit together in this work as one man, we must entertain each other in brotherly affection. [W]e must delight in each other, make others' conditions our own, rejoice together, mourn together, labor, and suffer together, always having before our eyes our commission and community in the work, our community as members of the same body.... We shall find that the God of Israel is among us, when ten of us shall be able to resist a thousand of our enemies, when he shall make us a praise and glory. [Then] men shall say of succeeding plantations: the Lord make it like that of New England.

For we must consider that we shall be as a city upon a hill. The eyes of all people are upon us, so that if we shall deal falsely with our God in this work we have undertaken and so cause him to withdraw his present help from us, we shall be made a story and a by-word through the world.... If our hearts shall turn away so that we will not obey... we shall surely perish out of the good land [even if] we pass over this vast sea to possess it. Therefore let us choose life, that we, and our seed, may live, by obeying his voice, and cleaving to him, for he is our life, and our prosperity.

NOVA BRITANNIA.

OFFERING MOST

Excellent fruites by Planting in
VIRGINIA.

Exciting all such as be well affected
to further the same.

LONDON
Printed for SAMVEL MACHAM, and are to be sold at
his Shop in Pauls Church-yard, at the
Signe of the Bul-head.
1 6 0 9.

This British broadside advertised economic opportunities to potential colonizers. Conversion of native Americans to Christianity attracted backers of the Virginia Company, but colonists focused on financial gain.

the colony's churches, which would excommunicate offenders and confiscate their property.

An emphasis on religion and moral order had been present in Virginia since its first settlement in 1607. The original charter of the Virginia Company declared that the company existed to propagate the "Christian religion to such people [Indians], as yet live in darkness and miserable ignorance of the true knowledge and worship of God." A 1610 tract advertising the colony insisted that it had Indian missions as its "principal and main ends…to recover out of the arms of the Devil, a number of poor and miserable souls, wrapped up unto death, in almost invincible ignorance."

It was not surprising, then, that the company sent 22 ministers to America before the colony went bankrupt in 1624. In 1616 the colony had no fewer than four ministers for only 350 settlers, a far higher ratio of clergymen to laity than could be found anywhere in England. The Virginia Company constructed a church in Jamestown with a cedar chancel and a black-walnut communion table. After Virginia became a royal colony in 1624 it legally established the Church of England and levied taxes to pay for churches and ministers "as near as may be to the Canons of England both in substance and circumstance."

Maryland, first settled in 1634, had similarly religious intentions but ones of a different persuasion. The colony was granted to the English Catholic convert George Calvert, Lord Baltimore, by King Charles I in 1632 and was understood to be a haven for persecuted English Catholics. Catholics had always formed a minority of the colony's settlers, and Calvert was sensitive to the realities of English public life. He instructed his brother Leonard, the colony's first governor, "to preserve unity and peace amongst all the passengers" to America. Maryland's Catholics would worship privately and were "to be silent upon all occasions of discourse concerning matters of religion." The governor was to "treat the Protestants with as much mildness and favor as justice will permit."

In the first decade, Maryland's Catholics established chapels for public worship, where Jesuit priests regularly performed Mass and held confession. The priests overcame fears of Indian reprisals among both the Catholic and Protestant settlers and began to carry out a systematic mission program among Maryland's Patuxent Indians. At the same time, Calvert resisted Jesuit pressure to increase their legal powers in the colony and allow them to purchase lands from the Indians independently, without the governor's explicit permission. In the end, Calvert won his arguments with the Jesuits, largely because they recognized that they were a minority in the colony and that the uneasy religious peace prevailing there might easily be short-lived.

George Calvert, Lord Baltimore established Maryland as a haven for persecuted English Catholics, although they were soon outnumbered there by Protestants, as they were in England.

By 1649, however, the year of John Winthrop's death in Massachusetts, the religious practices of the earliest English settlers everywhere in America diverged strongly from their founders' intentions. In New England the Puritans disagreed with each other, ignored new settlers, and lost their own religious intensity while becoming increasingly intolerant. In Virginia and Maryland the religious leadership failed, churches fell into disuse, Protestants attacked Catholics, and worship became so uncommon that many colonists observed it only occasionally. As a result, 17th-century American religious practices bore a surprisingly mottled face. In New England their early strength masked internal discord and then remarkable apathy. In the Chesapeake region the early religious fervor gave way to a spiritual lethargy that lasted well into the 1680s.

We are liable to misunderstand the Puritans partly because so many myths have come down to us about them: that they created a theocratic society—one ruled by ministers; that their religion stimulated unusual economic success; that they were mean and vindictive; and that they were perpetually unhappy. The early-20th-century social critic H. L. Mencken, who disliked the Puritans intensely, claimed they were driven by "the haunting fear that someone, somewhere, may be happy."

One way to grasp Puritanism is to understand what it was not. It never was a theocracy where ministers ruled a cowed laity. And Puritanism seems to have spurred no special economic gains. Except for the earliest years of settlement, New England probably was somewhat poorer than the Chesapeake region. Puritanism as a religion extended far beyond New England, to Presbyterians and Baptists in the middle and southern colonies. New England itself was not uniformly Puritan. By 1650 many New Englanders were paying little attention to Puritan demands and theology. Nor was Puritanism necessarily anti-intellectual and unbending. The Puritans danced and sang, and on occasion they even joked.

Puritanism was a rarefied form of Calvinism, the theology of the 16th-century Genevan reformer John Calvin. He stressed God's omnipotence, salvation by God's grace alone, and predestination, the idea that God has already determined who is to be saved and who not saved. Calvin's followers, including the English Puritans, added important ideas to Calvin's original formulations. In England they emphasized the quest for group discipline among believers organized into congregations, subjecting individuals to the censure of the congregations when they adopted wrong beliefs or behaved in immoral ways. In America they stressed the need for religious direction in the ongoing history of whole towns and communities, much in the way that John Winthrop had outlined in "A Model of Christian Charity."

Winthrop's ideals often played themselves out in the history of the New England towns, but not always in ways he imagined. Puritans settling there often signed "town covenants" that fused individual and community aims. The settlers of Dedham, Massachusetts, for example, established their community not merely as a place where individuals happened to purchase land but "in the fear and reverence of our Almighty God." They promised to "profess and practice one truth according to that most perfect rule, the foundation whereof is everlasting love." This covenant also meant that they agreed to exclude dissenters—a requirement that would soon be a problem—and to "receive only such unto us as may be probably of one heart with us."

In theory, the closed community advocated by Winthrop and established in towns like Dedham gave tremendous power to Puritan congregations. In 1631 the Massachusetts government, headed by Winthrop, required all voters to be members of the local Puritan congregation. As the Massachusetts assembly put it, the "body politic" would be synonymous with church members, and the civil government would be moral and virtuous, because it would be elected by good and right-minded citizens, all of whom belonged to Puritan churches. These congregations, which accepted the authority of no higher ecclesiastical body—hence their later labeling as "Congregationalist"—exercised the local management of congregational affairs. They did not form a democracy. Women could not vote at all in them, and power and authority within them tended to be held largely by wealthy, well-known men. But they became one of several different foundations of later American democracy.

The Puritans also worshipped—at great length—in ways that summarized their objections to the Church of England, England's state church. Puritans had two principal criticisms of Church of England, or Anglican, worship. First, Puritans objected to the many ceremonies, processions, and ornate music that characterized Anglican worship. Puritans searched the Scriptures but could find no specific warrant for these practices. (Catholics and Lutherans, in contrast, believed that such practices glorified God and were not specifically prohibited by the Scriptures.) Puritans therefore stripped their services of these age-old ceremonies and elaborate music. They emphasized prayer, Bible reading, psalm singing, and a sermon, which they believed constituted the only essential elements of early Christian worship. The Puritan objection to ornate music did not, however, preclude the singing of psalms to simple tunes without an organ or instrumental accompaniment. One person sometimes sang a line first—a technique called lining out—and the congregation followed. In a society where illiteracy was high, singing psalms was an important way to teach biblical lessons.

Second, Puritans objected to Anglican theology and doctrine, which was "Arminian" in character. It followed the theology of the 16th-century Dutch theologian Jacob Arminius, who modified Calvin's emphasis on predestination by stressing that men and women indeed made free choices that affected their salvation, although God knew about these choices in advance. In contrast, Puritans stressed the complete dependence of men and women upon God for salvation and rejected the idea that they could do anything on their own to achieve salvation. Men and women worshipped God because they were dependent upon God and obliged to worship him, not because they could win salvation by doing so.

In New England, as in England itself, Puritan worship was lengthy. It typically consisted of an opening prayer, a reading from the Bible, psalm singing, a sermon, another singing of a psalm, a prayer, and a concluding blessing. The entire service might last three to four hours. Although the opening prayer was relatively short, perhaps 15 minutes, the concluding prayer often lasted an hour, and in 1680 a Dutch traveler reported that one Massachusetts minister prayed for a "full two hours in length." The sermon, which also lasted an hour or more, customarily examined the biblical text read at the opening of the service.

Because of the intimacy of Puritan worship and community, some New England towns became "communities of saints." Congregations determined the values Christians should follow and watched, judged, and condemned those who strayed. In 1639 the Boston courts fined a Puritan merchant named Robert Keayne for profit gouging. Supplies from England were scarce, and Keayne had raised his prices to take advantage of market shortages. Rather than make "others' conditions our own," as Governor Winthrop had urged, Keayne had sought to profit from them, and the courts fined him for doing so. But Keayne then faced even more serious censure from his congregation. That body conducted an "exquisite search" of Keayne's behavior and condemned him again in front of his fellow church members. This judgment humiliated Keayne for the remainder of his life. It also illustrates the Puritans' affinity for censure and, sometimes, vindictiveness.

[12]

An Indians having Strong Drink in his Custody, (except Cyder made of Fruit of their own growth.) ibid.

The Drink to be siezed, for the Poor of the Town. And the Indian to be Examined before a Justice.

An Indians being Drunk. p. 63

A Fine of Five Shillings, for the Poor of the Town. Or, A Scourging, not exceeding Ten Lashes.

(XV.)

Off. Any Man being found in Bed with another mans Wife. p. 65

Pen. Both Man and Woman severely Scourged, (not exceeding Thirty Stripes.)

Unless it appear that one party was meerly surprized, and consented not; and then the Punishment of that party Abated.

Adultery Committed. p. 66.

Convicted before the Justices of Assize, - both Man and Woman to be set on the Gallowes an Hour, with a Rope about their Neck, and the other end cast over the Gallowes. And in the way from thence to the common Gaol, to be Scourged, not exceeding Forty Stripes. And forever after to wear a Capital A of two Inches long, of a contrary Colour to their

[13]

their Cloathes, sewed on their upper Garments, on the Back or Arm, in open view. And as often as they appear without it, openly to be Scourged, not exceeding Fifteen Stripes.

(XVI.)

Off. To Marry any other, the former Husband or Wife, being alive; (unless they have been absent for Three Years, and in this Term have not heard of one another.)

And except in Case of Divorce, or where the Marriage has been declared Void; or been made under the Age of Consent. p. 66.

Explanation 134.

Pen. Death, as in Cases of Felony; in whatever County the Offender is apprehended.

(XVII.)

Off. Retailers of Strong Drink, suffering People to sit drinking in their Houses, or their Dependences. Or Selling any other Drink, than what they have a License for. p. 74

Pen. The like Forfeitures as by Law inflicted on them that Sell without License.

Any Officers, taking a Bribe, to Conceal such Offences. ibid.

T.

> Puritans used the law to enforce morality, as in the law that required men and women convicted of adultery to wear "a Capital A of two inches long ... sewed on their upper Garments."

What especially distinguished New England's Puritans, at least briefly, was their willingness to attempt to do good even though they believed men and women were sinful and depraved. For a time, 17th-century New England Puritanism thrived on the tension produced by these conflicting aims and views. Michael Wigglesworth, a tutor at Harvard, struggled for years with his impulses and what he called his "carnal" habits: "I am often slothful and lay down the weapons of my warfare and do not fight, cry [and] strive as I should against them." Yet if anything he enjoyed this self-reproach, because it measured his labor as a sinful man trying to do good. Congregations acted similarly. It was not that these bodies were healthy because no one sinned. Rather, Puritanism's success depended on the way a congregation's members accepted censure, advice, and consolation, much as Robert Keayne had done. Only in this way could sinful Puritans be models for others and their communities.

In the end, Puritanism failed most notably when the men and women of New England drifted away from the discipline of the congregation and slowly, almost imperceptibly, abandoned the quest for a godly life that Puritan doctrine told them they were unlikely to achieve yet whose pursuit honored God even when it failed.

Puritanism also brought turmoil even within its own ranks. As early as 1636, less than a decade after the Puritans' arrival in Massachusetts, Boston witnessed an extraordinary trial that resulted in charges of heresy among the town's clergy and the expulsion of a prominent merchant and his wife from the community. The case centered on Anne Hutchinson, the wife of William Hutchinson, who had landed in Boston in 1634, fresh from the continuing persecution of Puritans in England. Before emigrating she had, for more than a decade in the 1620s and early 1630s, listened tenaciously to the sermons of the reforming minister John Cotton, who had already become a legend among England's Puritans. Cotton did away with much Church of England ritual and stressed preaching, concentrating on the idea that only God's grace, not paltry human works, led to salvation. Cotton fled England for America in 1633 after spending a year hiding from Archbishop William Laud, who threatened to imprison him for his reforming activities. This episode left Cotton's followers like Anne Hutchinson fearful and worried about their safety and religion. Now, safely arrived in Massachusetts, she felt she could continue Cotton's instruction in America.

Hutchinson's freedom in America soon dissolved, however, into argument, banishment, and death. By 1636, only two years after she arrived in Boston, most ministers were aghast at her behavior. Hutchinson had begun speaking about religious doctrine to groups of 60 to 80 men and women. She interpreted the Scriptures. Worse, she said that many Boston clergymen possessed "no gifts or graces." In 1637 the Boston authorities charged her with civil offenses, including "traducing [maligning] the ministers and their ministry." Her followers defended her by ridiculing the ministers and their English university training. Hutchinson, they said, "preaches better Gospel than any of your black-coats that have been at the Ninneversity."

Anne Hutchinson's trial demonstrated how assertive a Puritan woman could be. She directly challenged Governor John Winthrop when he interrogated her, saying, "What law have I broken?" She attacked "legal" preachers who stressed religious rules and regulations rather than God's free grace and salvation. She upbraided ministers who criticized her use of biblical citations when she defended her teaching: "Must I show my name written therein?" She claimed that men and women who were saved by God were not bound by the civil law as others were but obeyed it only as an example to the unsaved. And, most disastrously, she claimed that she spoke directly to God and possessed powers of "immediate revelation...by the voice of [God's] own spirit to my soul!" She needed no intermediaries, no unfit clergymen.

Hutchinson paid for her boldness. The Boston court banished her from Massachusetts for undermining the civil order. She moved to Rhode Island, where her husband died in 1642. A year later, Hutchinson and all but one of her six children were killed by Indians after she moved to north of New York City. Although Thomas Welde, a member of the court that convicted Hutchinson in Boston, later gloated that "God's hand" could be seen in Hutchinson's death, the affair cast a pall over Puritan New England. It demonstrated that a wide variety of beliefs could in fact be found among the Puritans and that achieving religious uniformity in Puritan New England might come at a very high price.

More serious problems stemmed from mundane causes. Although the number of Puritan congregations increased as towns grew up in the countryside, the percentage of church members in the towns began to decline, especially after about 1660. Many congregations turned inward, leaving new settlers outside the church. Spiritual vitality sagged. Second- and third-generation children lacked the experience with God and the knowledge of theology known to first-generation settlers. As a result, they were not admitted to the congregations, because they could not give a public accounting of "God's dealings" with them.

In the 1660s some, but not all, congregations adopted a "halfway covenant" to solve the membership problem. This agreement allowed the children of lagging second-generation parents to be baptized so that they would have a kind of "halfway" membership in their grandparents' congregations. But only the old settlers benefited from this innovation; new settlers who arrived from other towns or England never took up membership in the congregations.

Boston indeed became a "city on a hill," but not a city John Winthrop would have liked. By 1649, when Winthrop died only 20 years after the Puritans settled there, Boston was more modern than Puritan. More than half the town's adults ignored its churches and did not ask to belong to them. In Plymouth, to the south, children of the original settlers so often went away to pursue new lands and opportunities that the town minister, William Bradford, described Plymouth as "an ancient mother grown old and forsaken of her children." The town unity that Winthrop and Bradford so valued had fallen victim to individual economic enterprise.

Other towns took more relaxed views on the question of church membership and politics. Some allowed the unchurched and the landless to vote despite the colony's laws on the subject. Some of the other towns had as many unchurched residents as Boston. Still more never "owned" a town covenant or, if they did, plunged into bitter quarrels in which economics competed with religion. When the Rev. Edmund Brown led one faction against another in land allocation disputes in Sudbury, Massachusetts, the town officers finally warned him in the 1640s not to "meddle." They called his lobbying a "dishonor to God...a prejudice to his ministry" and "a hindrance to the conversion and building up of souls." Indeed, one resident simply told Brown that "setting aside your office, I regard you no more than another man." In short, Brown might be a clergyman, but many parishioners thought he had too much interest in land.

By the 1690s churches still were important in New England, and church members still dominated local and provincial politics. But society had changed. Many second- and third-generation New Englanders had lost their religious fervor. The new immigrants, from England, Scotland, and even France, did not join the older Puritan congregations. By 1690 many New England settlers did not belong to a Puritan congregation. Church membership that had been as high as 70 to 80 percent in the 1630s and 1640s plummeted to half those rates by the 1670s. In Salem, Massachusetts, only about 30 percent of the taxpayers belonged to the town's Puritan congregations in 1690, and in four Connecticut towns—New Haven, New London, Stonington, and Woodbury—only about 15 percent of the towns' men belonged to its churches by the 1680s.

New England also became more spiritually diverse. When the president of Harvard College, Henry Dunster, became a Baptist in 1654, leaders of the college forced him to resign. By 1670 Baptist, Presbyterian, and Quaker congregations all could be found in New England, often in competition with the old Puritan Congregational churches. French Protestant, or Huguenot, refugees set-tled in Rhode Island and Boston in the 1680s and shocked some Puritans, because these newcomers celebrated Christmas, which the Puritans did not. The Huguenots' arrival heralded more immigration by non-English set-tlers, such as the Scots, Scots-Irish, and the Welsh. And by 1695 even the hated old Church of England had estab-lished a congregation in Boston, although the town authorities had used every possible legal means to stop its formation.

Cotton Mather, New Eng-land's best-known Puritan clergyman at the end of the 17th century, worried about witchcraft and occult practices among English residents and backed the 1692 Salem witch trials.

News about the practice of magic also circulated in New England. An East Haven, Connecticut, man claimed he could "raise the Devil" and drew horoscopes for his neighbors. A wealthy Massachusetts woman claimed she had learned fortune-telling by reading William Lilly's astro-logical textbook *Christian Astrology,* published in London in 1643. By 1689 Cotton Mather acknowledged that disturbing numbers of New Englanders were employing magical practices to cure diseases, even though they knew, or should have known, that in doing so they were invoking the aid of the devil.

Little wonder, then, that New England's authorities were increasingly prosecuting witches in the late 17th century. These trials culminated in the infamous Salem witch trials of 1692, in which 20 people were execut-ed, another 150 arrested, and many more privately accused and gossiped about. Whereas witch trials were uncommon in England after 1645, in New England the number of witch trials rose dramatically between 1660 and 1690, prompted in part by a need for scapegoats to explain the decline of "traditional" Puritan values, the rise of religious diversity, and people's resorting to magic. Surely the devil had brought these upon New England.

The Salem witch trials of 1692 capped the rise of witch trials in New England after 1660 but then brought the trials and some Puritan supporters into disrepute when public reaction turned against the execution of alleged witches. The episode in question began when local girls accused an Indian slave, Tituba, of casting spells. This accusation, pursued by the local minister, Rev. Samuel Parris, escalated after Tituba named several local women as witches. Then the afflicted girls identified more women and several men as witches based on "spectral evidence"—evidence that came from the "specters" or ghostly apparitions of accused witches that appeared in dreams of the afflicted.

Some of the girls' behavior was merely innocuous, if odd. Twelve-year-old Ann Putnam, for example, called out to Reverend Parris in the church, "There is a yellow bird sitting on the minister's hat, as it hangs on the pin in the pulpit." But other accusations were vicious, involving curses and suggestions of sexual impropriety and desire. According to Reverend Parris and other New England ministers, such as Boston's Cotton Mather, the accused witches made bargains with the devil, luring the young girls with promises of punishing their enemies or finding them wealthy husbands. The witches seemed to exemplify the threat to New England's Christianity, its society, and its values.

In fact, personal tensions and social cleavages played important roles in the accusations. Reverend Parris was a weak, ineffective minister who used the witchcraft accusations to assert his own power and explain his failings. Some of the accused men owned large tracts of land desired by competing families, and some of the accused women had long been disliked in the community. Despite adamant denials by the women and men indicted at Salem, by September the courts had hanged 14 women and 5 men for witchcraft and pressed one man to death with stones because he challenged the court's authority and refused to plead guilty or innocent to witchcraft charges.

The excesses of the trials proved their own undoing, however, and probably saved lives later, if not in 1692. Initially, the convictions and hangings brought only more accusations. By October 1692 more than 150 people stood accused of witchcraft. But now the accusations reached people who seemed unlikely to be witches yet who had been seen as witch "specters" in dreams. Long-standing criticism of spectral evidence that had been pushed aside in the first trials suddenly seemed more relevant. Boston's Rev. Increase Mather, whose son Cotton Mather had earlier backed the witch trials, disavowed spectral evidence and called for an end to the trials. Governor William Phipps disbanded the special court he had established to conduct the trials, and no further witch trials and executions for witchcraft occurred in New England.

Over the next 15 years Puritan leaders grappled with their failures at Salem. By 1696 the Boston judge Samuel Sewall, who had sat on the Salem court, publicly confessed his errors. In 1700 a Boston merchant named Robert Calef denounced Cotton Mather and the New England clergy in his book *More Wonders of the Invisible World.* In it he accused them not only of vanity but of stupidity. After all, he argued, if the devil was so clever, couldn't he inflame wrongful accusations as well as entice women and men into witchcraft? In 1714 the Massachusetts assembly reversed the convictions of those accused and executed at Salem and called upon the colony to repent for its delusions.

If the Puritans never succeeded in creating a peaceful established religion in New England, they did produce an important preaching style that resonated through America well into the 19th century, the so-called jeremiad sermon. Broadly speaking, the theme of the jeremiad, which was styled after the laments and prophecies of doom in the Old Testament's "Lamentations of Jeremiah," was the decline of spiritual fervor among the citizenry, the community's flirtation with disaster, and its dramatic

Samuel Sewall of Boston presided over the 1692 Salem witch trials but apologized for his actions in 1696, "asking pardon of men" for his misdeeds.

recovery. Although no golden age of Puritanism ever existed in New England, as Anne Hutchinson's troubles in the 1630s demonstrate, ministers used this kind of sermon to promote church membership, though with limited success.

Long after the Puritans had disappeared, however, the jeremiad style provided an important rhetorical form invoked in times of crisis to decry the country's sins and call down judgment upon them. By claiming in his second inaugural address in March 1865 that slavery was "one of those offenses" that God "now wills to remove" and quoting Psalm 19 that "the judgments of the Lord are true and righteous altogether," President Abraham Lincoln invoked the jeremiad style of sermonizing to shame Americans into greater resolve and purpose in pursuing the Civil War.

Religion fared quite differently in the Chesapeake region. For a time in the 1620s and early 1630s, Virginia's ministers and congregations tried to maintain vigorous worship and moral discipline in the colony. The Virginia House of Burgesses established many parishes, some of which constructed church buildings. The ministers published public notices of marriages ("banns"), and church wardens cited settlers for not observing the Sabbath, such as "Thomas Farley, Gentleman," who missed worship for three months. They shamed women convicted of sexual misdeeds by ordering them to dress in white gowns, hold white wands, and stand on chairs or stools during public worship. In some congregations, worshipers publicly confessed their sins and sought forgiveness much as they did in New England.

Indeed, Puritan-style congregations emerged in the area south of Jamestown, in Nansemond and Lower Norfolk counties, in the 1640s. In 1641 more than 70 men and women signed a letter to the New Haven Puritan minister John Davenport pleading for Puritan clergymen to move to Virginia to serve their congregations. Three New England ministers did in fact arrive to serve the Virginia congregations, but they were gone by 1650. Governor William Berkeley saw them as a threat to the established Church of England and not only forced them to leave Virginia but made many of their supporters move across the Chesapeake Bay to Maryland.

Yet the greatest threat to Virginia's Church of England in particular and Christian worship in general was organizational shortcoming, not Puritan competition. The Church of England failed to sustain working parishes and congregations despite its establishment as the colony's official church. Most Virginia counties never added congregations as their populations expanded, and as early as the 1650s many Virginians did not live within easy reach of a congregation with regular services. The congregations that did exist often did not keep their church buildings in repair, and many churches lacked ministers. Worshipers sometimes met in homes and barns, but this worship was not always sustained. A 1656 description of Virginia depicted the colony's Anglican ministers as drunkards who "battle in a pulpit, roar in a tavern,...[and] by their dissoluteness destroy rather than feed their flocks." Perhaps it was just as well, then, when a 1661 pamphlet claimed that only 10 of Virginia's 50 parishes actually had resident clergymen.

A few of the clergy struggled on against the rising tide of parish vacancies and ministerial sloth. In Accomack County, on Virginia's eastern shore, Thomas Teackle served several parishes, apparently well, for more than 40 years between his arrival before 1652 and his death in 1695, making him the longest-serving minister in 17th-century Virginia. He argued about his salary with several parish vestries, the board of laymen who managed parish affairs, and when he died he was one of the wealthiest clergymen in colonial America, worth 337 pounds sterling, not counting his land and slaves (he owned 11 at his death). Teackle preached regularly, not only Sabbath after Sabbath but for funerals as well: in 1679 one settler asked not only that his friends refrain from drunkenness at his funeral but that "Mr. Teackle if possible preach my funeral sermon."

Little wonder. Teackle could draw upon an enormous library when writing his sermons, the largest known in 17th-century Virginia and far larger than most Puritan libraries—more than 300 books on biblical commentary, Puritanism, Anglicanism, medicine, and humor, as well as many occult titles that mixed highly learned or speculative magic with Christianity. But Thomas Teackle ministered to only one small part of

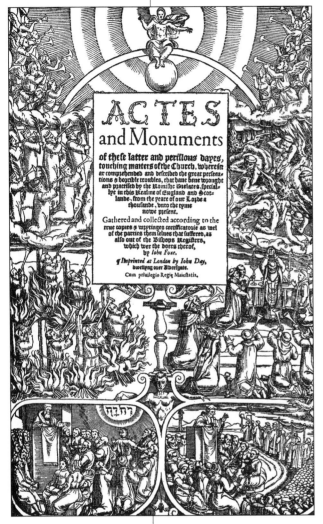

John Foxe's *Actes and Monuments* or *Book of Martyrs*, published in many 17th-century editions, castigated Catholics and helped stimulate popular English anti-Catholicism that drove Catholic worship underground in Maryland after 1650.

Virginia, and no one else duplicated his life and achievement in the colony before 1690.

The situation in Maryland was little better, despite the colony's seemingly promising start as a haven for persecuted English Catholics. Owned by George Calvert, Lord Baltimore, England's most prestigious Catholic nobleman, Maryland attracted practicing Catholics who saw in America a chance to remain English yet practice a faith forbidden at home. Priests accompanied these settlers; by the early 1640s Catholicism offered the principal form of public Christian worship available in the colony, with four Catholic church buildings erected there by 1650.

But English anti-Catholicism quickly destroyed public Catholic worship in the colony. Political disturbances and revolts in 1645, 1654, 1676, and 1689 arose as major outbreaks of anti-Catholic violence by non-Catholic settlers contesting Lord Baltimore's power in the colony. They attacked Catholic church buildings and forced priests to return to England. In one episode, anti-Catholic rioters threw prayer books out of a barn while yelling, "Burn them Papists' Devils," equating the Pope with the Devil. From the 1650s until the eve of the American Revolution, Maryland's Catholics usually worshipped privately in homes rather than publicly in church buildings, and only a few Catholic priests conducted worship in the colony between 1660 and the 1740s.

Little Protestant worship supplanted the disappearing Catholic services until the 1690s. A quarter century before the settlement of Quaker Pennsylvania, a female Quaker preacher, Elizabeth Harris, preached in

Maryland in 1655, and slowly several Quaker meetings were formed there. But as late as 1690 the Quakers probably counted fewer than 500 adherents in the colony. Some Virginia Puritans exiled to Maryland by Governor Berkeley in 1650 established a Presbyterian congregation in the colony, but it seems to have disappeared quickly. By the 1670s, then, Maryland probably knew only one or two Catholic priests and, at best, one or two Protestant clergymen in the colony. It is no wonder that in the 1680s a Church of England minister, John Yeo, wrote that Maryland was a place where "the Lord's day is profaned, religion despised, and all notorious vices committed…it is become a Sodom of uncleanness and a pest house of iniquity."

By the 1680s the Virginia and Maryland colonies had become remarkably indifferent in matters of religion. Settlers there seldom participated in public Christian worship and many children grew to adulthood without Christian baptism. Some 85 percent of the children born in Charles Parish, Virginia, between 1649 and 1680 never received baptism in the Church of England, and since no dissenting Protestants were active in the parish, it is doubtful that they were baptized anywhere else. In Maryland's Kent County only 5 baptisms occurred among 115 white children born between 1657 and 1670. A French Jesuit reported that English settlers in Maryland had gone so long without receiving the rite of baptism that they had stopped complaining about it.

Funerals in Maryland bore an especially secular character between 1640 and 1690. Owing to the lack of ministers, priests, and church buildings, raucous banquets became the dominant public ceremony surrounding death. Meats, fowl, breads, cakes, cider, and as many casks of brandy, rum, and beer as the deceased's estate could afford were spread among surviving friends in drunken parties that lasted two or three days. In 1662 the Charles County court complained that it was not "Christian like" when neighbors turned "their bousing [drinking] Cups to the quantity of three barrels of beer" worth "nine hundred pounds of tobacco." The neighbors

This crude anti-Catholic drawing, "The Pope, or Man of SIN," appeared in the *New England Primer* in 1737 and described the evil in various parts of the Pope's body, such as "In his feet, swiftness to shed blood," or "In his heart, Malice, Murder, and Treachery."

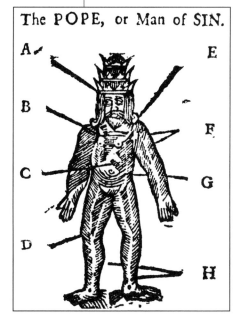

The POPE, or Man of SIN.

The 1649 Maryland Act of Toleration did not grant religious toleration to everyone but did permit religious worship among an unprecedented number of Protestants and even Catholics in early Maryland.

A LAW
OF
MARYLAND
Concerning
RELIGION.

Forasmuch as in a well-governed and Christian Commonwealth, Matters concerning Religion and the Honour of God ought to be in the first place to be taken into serious consideration, and endeavoured to be settled. Be it therefore Ordained and Enacted by the Right Honourable CÆCILIUS Lord Baron of Baltemore, absolute Lord and Proprietary of this Province, with the Advice and Consent of the Upper and Lower House of this General Assembly, That whatsoever person or persons within this Province and the Islands thereunto belonging, shall from henceforth blaspheme GOD, that is curse him; or shall deny our Saviour JESUS CHRIST to be the Son of God; or shall deny the Holy Trinity, the Father, Son, & Holy Ghost; or the Godhead of any of the said Three Persons of the Trinity, or the Unity of the Godhead, or shall use or utter any reproachful speeches, words, or language, concerning the Holy Trinity, or any of the said three Persons thereof, shall be punished with death, and confiscation or forfeiture of all his or her Lands and Goods to the Lord Proprietary and his Heirs.

should instead have showed "a mournfulness for the loss of their friend," the court observed. But few heeded the plea.

Magic came to the Chesapeake as it had to New England. In 1626 the Virginia courts investigated magical acts performed by Goodwife Wright. She allegedly used magic to help neighbors turn curses back upon those who had pronounced them, predicted the deaths of neighbors, made a woman and her newborn infant sick, caused a hunter to miss when shooting deer, and made a servant girl "dance stark naked." One woman with a mean husband was consoled by Wright's advice to "be content, for thou shall shortly bury him." (In fact, the man died soon afterward.)

Other Virginians nailed horseshoes over their doors to protect themselves from alleged witches. Some claimed that witches ruined their tobacco; one man described to a Virginia court how a witch "had rid him along the Seaside and home to his own house." Even the clergyman Thomas Teackle owned books about the occult arts. These works described magic, alchemy (in which magic was used to try to transform base metals like lead into gold), and astrology, sometimes to cure diseases. One of the books in Teackle's library, Marin Cureau de la Chambre's *The Art How to Know Men,* published in London in 1675, employed astrology, chiromancy (palm reading), and metoposcopy (forehead reading) to analyze human passions.

By the 1690s the religious future of British America worried many observers. Puritan writers like Boston's Cotton Mather—although they tended to exaggerate the achievements of the earliest Puritan settlers—believed that their own generation was not living up to the models set by their parents and grandparents. Settlers in Maryland and Virginia found themselves bereft of spiritual guidance and leadership and seldom could carry on worship on their own. The next century, however, would see the rise of new patterns of religious activity, including new religious groups and beliefs. Not only would religious life be transformed in New England and the Chesapeake region—a new religious order would be created everywhere in British America, extending as far as the many new settlements that strengthened the European presence throughout the land.

To learn about occult arts such as palm reading or astrology, colonists could consult Marin Cureau de la Chambre's *The Art How to Know Men* and other books like it.

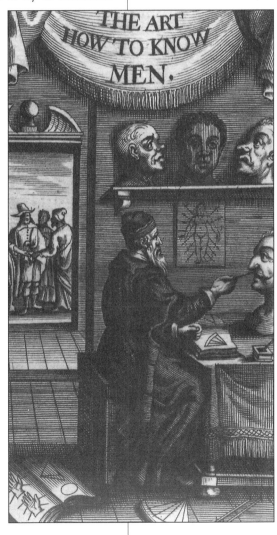

The Singing Choir, 1 Ludwig Miller, 2 John Barnitz, 3 George Snyder, 4 Christopher Stöchr, 5 Daniel Lauman, 6 Lewis Shive, 7 William Hornschild, 8 George Barnitz, 9 Steffe Horn, 10 George Miller, 11 Michael Eurich, 12 mis Herman, 13 mis Laub, mis Stöchr, 14 mis Cramer, 15 Mis Hay, 16 the Organist John Morris, Charles Fisher. Pastor, Rev. Jacob Goering,

In Side of the old Lutheran Church in 1800, York, Pa.

Chapter 3

The Flowering of Religious Diversity

Thomas Dongan was perplexed. In 1683 he had become governor of New York, the old Dutch colony that the British had conquered in 1664. Dongan was a Roman Catholic who keenly felt the desirability of religious tolerance. But he had never encountered such religious diversity as he had found in New York. When he arrived from England 1683, he expected to find one or two ministers of the Dutch Reformed Church, the Protestant state church of the Netherlands, and a Church of England minister preaching to the small but growing English population in New York.

Instead, Dongan encountered a religious blend so rich and confusing that he hardly knew what to make of it. The Dutch Reformed Church was indeed the town's largest congregation; Dongan observed that there were "not many of the Church of England, [and] few Roman Catholics." But New York teemed with other groups. It harbored an "abundance of Quaker preachers and women [preachers] especially." It contained "singing Quakers" and "ranting Quakers" who did not always see eye to eye. "Sabbatarian" and "Antisabbatarian" Baptists disagreed about which day was the true Sabbath; some worshiped on Saturday, others on Sunday. New Englanders who had already migrated to New York divided themselves between the traditional Puritans and the Baptists. Jews from

Lutheran services in 18th-century Pennsylvania were not always as crowded as they are depicted in this drawing made about 1800, but they probably were full of surprises, such as unleashed dogs.

Curaçao in the Dutch West Indies gave the town a distinctive non-Christian element. Yet most New Yorkers did not belong to a religious congregation at all, despite the wide variety of available choices. They were like the religiously indifferent in Europe, though they seemed more visible in New York. In short, Dongan wrote, "of all sorts of opinion there are some, and the most part [are] of none at all."

New York prefigured the religious future of 18th-century America. In colonial America many religions, not just one or two, quickly came to typify the immigrants' spiritual life, and much of this diversity emerged between 1690 and 1770. Congregational statistics measured the growth of religious diversity in the colonies. Before 1690, 90 percent of all congregations in colonial America were either Congregationalist (as in Puritan New England) or Anglican (as in Virginia). But by 1770 this was no longer true. Congregationalism and the Church of England indeed remained strong on the eve of the American Revolution. About 20 percent of all colonial congregations were Congregationalist and about 15 percent adhered to the Church of England. But by 1770 Scottish and Scots-Irish Presbyterians made up 18 percent of all colonial congregations, English and Welsh Baptists about 15 percent, and Quakers, German Lutherans, and German Reformed each claimed 5 to 10 percent of the colonial congregations. Non-English congregations by then accounted for at least 25 percent of all colonial congregations, although they had been rare before 1690, and by 1770 no single religious body could claim more than 20 percent of all the colonial congregations.

The "middle colonies" of New York, New Jersey, Pennsylvania, and Delaware proved especially diverse and, ultimately, good prophets of America's religious future. By the Revolution, the middle colony congregations were divided among the Presbyterians, German Lutherans, German Reformed, Quakers, Dutch Reformed, Anglicans, Mennonites, Moravians, Catholics, German Baptists, and the newest and smallest of all the groups, English Methodists. At most, Presbyterians claimed 20 percent of the middle colony congregations, with the many additional denominations dividing the remaining 80 percent. By the time of the American Revolution, then, religious diversity had become one of the

A French immigrant, Peter Manigault, entertains well-dressed company in his South Carolina home in the 1760s. Some French Huguenots who fled France for religious reasons in the 1680s achieved great wealth in America.

region's most distinctive features and, in fact, a major component of colonial life everywhere.

Three causes stimulated European religious pluralism in the American colonies after 1690: the immigration of Europeans from many different religious groups, the expansion of religious groups already present earlier but in only small numbers, and a surprising persistence of beliefs in magic and occultism long after the infamous Salem witch trials of 1692. These three causes together produced a religious diversity unmatched in any Old World society.

Protestants from France, or Huguenots, became the first significant non-English Protestants to arrive in the colonies at the end of the 17th century. They fled France in the 1680s when the French king, Louis XIV, revoked the Edict of Nantes, proclaimed in 1598, that had given the Huguenots limited freedom to worship. More than 100,000 Huguenots left France, and between 2,000 and 2,500 finally reached the British colonies in America between 1680 and 1700. Most Huguenots came to America because they could not return to France and because their life in Europe's Huguenot refugee centers was frequently miserable. In London, for example, Huguenots had little work, few possessions, and poor prospects.

In America, the Huguenots settled primarily in Boston, New York, and South Carolina. But after forming new congregations they quickly assimilated or mixed with English and other European settlers. They usually took up occupations similar to those of the settlers around them. In Boston, New York City, and Charleston the Huguenots became merchants and artisans. In rural New York and low country South Carolina they became farmers and planters. In their rural settlements they quickly embraced slaveholding, whether in northern farming villages like New Rochelle, New York, or in rural South Carolina. Even though they had fled France to preserve their own freedom, they could not resist the economic opportunities offered by the cheap labor of enslaved Africans.

The Huguenots also assimilated into their surrounding culture in matters of family life and religion. They married non-Huguenots quickly. As early as 1710, only 20 years after they had arrived, more than half of all Huguenots took non-Huguenot wives and husbands. They joined other religious congregations, becoming Congregationalists in Boston and Anglicans, Dutch Reformed, Presbyterians, and Quakers in New York, and Anglicans and sometimes Baptists in South Carolina. By 1750 only two small Huguenot congregations still existed in the colonies, in New York City and Charleston, and both closed at the time of the American Revolution.

The German-speaking immigrants, who accounted for the largest number of settlers arriving from continental Europe, came out of at least six different religious traditions: Lutherans, German Reformed, Mennonites, Moravians, German Baptists, and Catholics. These Germans settled principally in Pennsylvania, but substantial numbers of other German immigrants also resided in New York, Maryland, western Virginia, and North Carolina. In all, as many as 75,000 Germans probably immigrated to the British colonies between 1700 and 1776.

The German Lutherans and German Reformed immigrants claimed the largest proportion of the German immigrants to America. The Lutheran Church was the largest German immigrant church, especially in Pennsylvania. Lutheranism was the principal state-supported Protestant church in many of the German states and had a larger following than any

A late-18th-century German Lutheran minister in Pennsylvania baptizes a baby surrounded by its parents and sponsors. Religious rituals such as baptism helped cement a sense of community among the participants.

other Protestant denomination in German-speaking Europe. This meant that in most northern German parishes children would be baptized as Lutherans as a matter of course, even if their parents were not especially loyal church members.

Several Lutheran congregations were formed among the German immigrants in New York and Pennsylvania in the 1690s. These added to the two or three Swedish Lutheran congregations in Delaware that remained there from the short-lived colony of New Sweden. (Settled in 1638, New Sweden had been captured by the Dutch in 1655.) More German Lutheran congregations were organized in the 1710s and 1720s as German immigration increased. But little leadership was present until minister Henry Melchior Muhlenberg arrived in Philadelphia in 1742. Guided by the motto "Ecclesia plantanda" ("Let the church be planted"), Muhlenberg traveled about Pennsylvania for three decades, organizing congregations, chastising religiously indifferent immigrants, and disciplining wayward clergymen in an effort to overcome low attendance and loose manners among immigrants, most of whom had come to America for secular rather than religious reasons.

The German Reformed Church constituted the second-largest church of German-speaking immigrants in America. German Reformed immi-

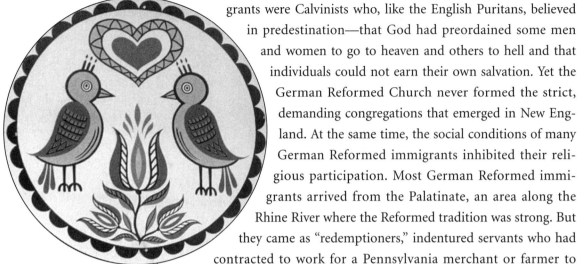

Pennsylvania Dutch farmers decorated their barns, furniture, and important documents with colorful geometric designs known as hex signs. A sign like this might have appeared on a marriage certificate, with the heart symbolizing love, the birds, good luck and happiness, and the tulip, faith.

grants were Calvinists who, like the English Puritans, believed in predestination—that God had preordained some men and women to go to heaven and others to hell and that individuals could not earn their own salvation. Yet the German Reformed Church never formed the strict, demanding congregations that emerged in New England. At the same time, the social conditions of many German Reformed immigrants inhibited their religious participation. Most German Reformed immigrants arrived from the Palatinate, an area along the Rhine River where the Reformed tradition was strong. But they came as "redemptioners," indentured servants who had contracted to work for a Pennsylvania merchant or farmer to "redeem" the cost of their ship passage, usually over a term of four years. Their labor for strangers, who were often English, and the absence of strong family and kinship ties among many such immigrants hindered their religious activity in the New World.

Several German "sectarian" groups also arrived in the colonies after 1690. The sects kept to themselves, restricted marriage to other members of the sect, and avoided close contact with nonmembers, whether German or English. They stressed a contemplative life, emphasized personal piety and spiritual reflection, rejected political involvement, and were pacifists who refused to fight in wars. Mennonites were present in the earliest German immigration to Pennsylvania in the 1680s. Followers of a 16th-century religious leader, Menno Simons, they settled first in Germantown, just outside Philadelphia, but after 1710 they established themselves largely in Lancaster County in central Pennsylvania, later called Pennsylvania Dutch country, a corruption of the word *Deutsche* or German. There, between 1720 and 1740, they were joined by followers of a Mennonite dissident from Switzerland, Jacob Amman, who demanded greater discipline and shunned those who rejected it, calling themselves the Amish in honor of their founder.

German "Dunkers," or members of the Church of the Brethren, originated as a dissident group within the German Reformed Church. They were called Dunkers in derision because they believed in baptism by full immersion in water, often in a river. The printer Christopher Sauer was the best-known Dunker in Pennsylvania. Sauer printed the first German-language newspaper in Pennsylvania in 1739 and produced an edition of Martin Luther's Bible in 1743, the first Bible printed in the American colonies. Another offshoot of the German Baptists established an ascetic perfectionist community at Ephrata in Lancaster County in the 1740s. This community separated men and women, observed Saturday as the Sabbath, and enjoyed considerable prosperity and success until internal disputes weakened it in the 1770s.

A German-speaking group usually called Moravians, because they originated in Moravia, the central region of the modern Czech Republic, also emigrated to the British colonies in the eighteenth century. Formally

Moravians received new members as "brothers" and "sisters" in ceremonies that separated men from women.

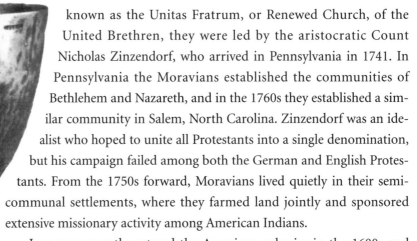

Paul Revere made this silver ceremonial cup for Moses Michael Hays, a member of Boston's small colonial Jewish community.

known as the Unitas Fratrum, or Renewed Church, of the United Brethren, they were led by the aristocratic Count Nicholas Zinzendorf, who arrived in Pennsylvania in 1741. In Pennsylvania the Moravians established the communities of Bethlehem and Nazareth, and in the 1760s they established a similar community in Salem, North Carolina. Zinzendorf was an idealist who hoped to unite all Protestants into a single denomination, but his campaign failed among both the German and English Protestants. From the 1750s forward, Moravians lived quietly in their semi-communal settlements, where they farmed land jointly and sponsored extensive missionary activity among American Indians.

Jews permanently entered the American colonies in the 1680s and 1690s. The first Jews in the American colonies, who arrived in New Amsterdam in 1654, came from Brazil. They were refugees who had fled that country after the Portuguese had captured the Dutch colony there. However, most of these immigrants left New Amsterdam within a few years. More permanent Jewish settlers arrived in the 1680s, and by 1695 they formed the first permanent synagogue in New York City, later called Shearith Israel (Remnant of Israel).

By the 1720s New York City (as New Amsterdam was now called) contained at least 20 Jewish families, who constituted about 2 percent of the town's population. In 1730 services at Shearith Israel moved from a rented building to the first permanent Jewish synagogue building in the colonies. Jews subsequently settled in Philadelphia, Charleston, Savannah, and Newport, Rhode Island, where the famous Touro Synagogue building, dedicated in 1763, has become the oldest surviving synagogue in the United States.

The colonial Jewish communities were small, located entirely in urban areas, and sometimes proved fragile. Most early Jewish immigrants were "Sephardic" Jews, who spoke Spanish or Portuguese and observed the traditions of worship of Spanish and Portuguese Judaism. Others were "Ashkenazic" Jews, German- or Yiddish-speaking Jews who observed the somewhat different rituals of northern and eastern Europe. Their small numbers made colonial Jews especially vulnerable to anti-Semitism, which came in various forms, from legal prohibitions against voting to public derision and occasional violence. Yet this kind of anti-Semitism was mild by comparison to that in Europe. European legal restrictions on Jews were far more severe and Jews were openly persecuted, not only in Spain and Portugal (from which they were expelled in 1492) but throughout Britain, France, and Germany.

Sometimes, however, it was difficult to preserve one's Jewish identity in the colonies. Abigail Franks was devastated when her daughter, Phila, secretly married Oliver DeLancey, son of a wealthy Huguenot merchant

The Ten Commandments adorn the wall of this reconstruction of the interior of Touro Synagogue in Newport, Rhode Island, built in 1763. In the New World, colonial craftsmen, following 18th-century British design, could create elegant places of worship.

A Mother Laments Her
Daughter's Faithlessness

The ethnic pluralism and relatively open religious toleration of colonial New York saw many colonists take brides and grooms from other religious faiths. Huguenots married Anglicans, Dutch Reformed married Quakers, and English Baptists married English Presbyterians. Yet mixed marriages could also cause anguish.

In this remarkable letter from Abigail Franks, wife of New York City merchant Jacob Franks, both of whom were Ashkenazic or German Jews, Abigail reports to her son Naphtali (whom she calls by the affectionate nickname Heartsey) in London the shocking news of her daughter Phila's secret marriage to wealthy Anglican Oliver DeLancey in New York City sometime in January 1743.

Flatbush Tuesday June 7th 1743

Dear Heartsey

I am now retired from Town and would from myself if it were possible to have some peace of mind from the severe affliction I am under on the conduct of that unhappy girl [Phila]. Good God what a shock it was when they acquainted me she had left the house and had been married six months. I can hardly hold my pen whilst I am a writing it. It's what I never could have imagined especially after what I heard her so often say that no consideration in life should ever induce her to disoblige such good parents.

I had heard the report of her going to be married to Oliver DeLancey, but as such reports had often been of either of your sisters I gave no heed to it further than a general caution of her conduct, which has always been unblemished. And is so still

in the eye of the Christians who allow she has disobliged us but has in no way been dishonorable being married to a man of worth and character.

My spirits was for some time so depressed that it was a pain to me to speak or see anyone. I have overcome it so far as not to make my concern so conspicuous, but I shall never have that serenity nor peace within I have so happily had hitherto. My house has been my prison ever since. I had not heart enough to go near the street door. It's a pain to me to think of going again to town, and if your father's business would permit him to live out of it, I never would go near it again....

Your Affectionate Mother

Abigail Franks

The first Methodist congregation in New York City, founded in 1768, worshiped in this building on John Street.

named Stephen DeLancey, in New York City in 1743. (The DeLanceys had already left the Huguenot Church and joined the Church of England.) She wrote her oldest son, then in London, "My spirits was for some time so depressed that it was a pain to me to speak or see anyone....My house has been my prison ever since. I had not heart enough to go near the street door." In fact, between 80 and 90 percent of colonial Jews married other Jews. But the Franks family intermarried with non-Jewish colonists so frequently that by the 1790s it had disappeared as a Jewish family in America.

The Methodists were the last new English religious group to arrive in the colonies. John and Charles Wesley began the Methodist reform movement in the Church of England in the 1740s. The movement drew its name from the Wesleys' emphasis on a "method" of regular prayer, devotional reading, and contemplation that drew participants closer to God and led to a personal experience of religious conversion. The Wesleys were Arminians, followers of the 16th-century Dutch theologian Jacob Arminius. They stressed the completeness of Christ's sacrifice for all men and women, rejecting Calvin's views about human depravity and his concept of predestination. Methodists believed that a combination of God's grace and human endeavor could pull believing Christians toward God. The Wesleys were influenced by Moravian missionaries working in England, and in 1738 John Wesley sought spiritual guidance from the Moravian leader Count Nicholas Zinzendorf in Germany.

The Wesleys first sent missionaries to the American colonies in 1769 even as the colonists' political contests with Parliament were still simmering. The early missionaries, led by Francis Asbury, worked in Maryland and Delaware as well as in New York City. The Methodists formed small "classes," usually involving a dozen or so believers, who used their meetings to deepen their spiritual life and commitment. Despite early success in attracting followers, especially poorer farmers in the countryside and laborers in cities like Annapolis, Philadelphia, and New York, the movement halted abruptly with the issuing of the Declaration of Independence in 1776. The Wesleys still worked within the Church of England, were politically conservative and deeply sensitive to charges of radicalism in their movement, and vigorously backed the Crown in its struggle with the colonies. In 1776 Wesley recalled all the Methodist missionaries in the colonies, and all of them except Francis Asbury returned to England. By the start of the Revolution, then, the first Methodist success in America seemed wasted.

The period from 1690 to 1770 also witnessed the dramatic growth of English, Scottish, and Welsh religious groups that had been present earlier in the colonies only in small numbers. The Quakers were among the most prominent and distinctive of these groups. The Society of Friends originated in England in the 1650s. They were derisively called Quakers because, as they said themselves, they "trembled at the Word of the Lord" and sometimes shook or "danced" during their religious services. Quaker services contained no hymns, formal sermons, or traditional liturgy and processions. Instead, individual Quakers described God's dealing with their souls and their struggles with moral and religious problems.

Led by George Fox, the Quakers believed that Christian revelation did not stop with the writing of the Bible and could be obtained in modern times. They believed that each individual possessed an "inward light" that, properly cultivated, might lead to religious truth. Attacked by both the government and other religious groups, the Quakers also became pacifists and refused to resist these assaults physically or fight in wars.

The settlement of Pennsylvania, acquired by the wealthy Quaker William Penn in 1681, transformed the Quaker presence in America. In fact, Quakers had begun seeking converts in the American colonies as early as the late 1650s. Successful Quaker preaching in Massachusetts, Rhode Island, and Maryland attracted small numbers of followers there and encouraged George Fox to visit Maryland, Virginia, and North Carolina in 1672 and 1673 and establish more meetings. These trips were difficult. In Maryland, Fox was "dirtied with getting through bogs," as he wrote in his journal. But his efforts always brought rewards—he won over, for example, "several magistrates with their wives, many Protestants of divers sorts, and some Papists [Catholics] and persons of chief account in the country."

Penn's acquisition of Pennsylvania, stimulated by earlier Quaker migration to New Jersey, turned Quakerism into a powerful religious force in the middle colonies. By 1685, only a few years after Pennsylvania began to be settled, so many thousands of Quakers had fled England to settle in Penn's new American territory that some Quaker authorities in England criticized his venture. Quaker churchmen in Wales complained in 1698 that "runnings to Pennsylvania" were stripping their meetings of members, and Quaker preachers became discouraged and found "cause to complain" about Penn's all-too-successful American colony.

In Pennsylvania and parts of New Jersey, Quakers dominated both government and society, in sharp contrast to their status in England as a persecuted minority. Although Pennsylvania became famous as a haven for many different religious and ethnic groups, the Quakers probably remained the colony's largest religious group into the 1720s. For decades they were Pennsylvania's most powerful and important merchants and farmers. They controlled the colony's politics until the mid-1750s, even though they were pacifists who opposed fighting, and this became a difficult principle to uphold when western settlers wanted protection from Indian attacks. The Quakers invented the first modern political party in the American colonies and through the famous "Quaker party" ran candidates for public office, including the Pennsylvania Assembly.

By the 1750s, however, the Quakers had become a minority in Pennsylvania, outnumbered by recent German, Scottish, and Scots-Irish immigrants. They also lost much of their own discipline as Quakers married non-Quakers; others traded in slaves and even in guns and munitions. Quaker politicians found it difficult to resist demands to meet Indian attacks on the Pennsylvania frontier with force. Reformers within the Quaker movement challenged Friends, including Quaker politicians, to return to older values. The reformers forced many, but not all, Quakers to withdraw from elective politics. They also increased the discipline in Quaker meetings and disowned Quakers with non-Quaker spouses or those who traded in slaves and guns. After 1750 the Quakers still remained important in Pennsylvania and New Jersey, but they no longer dominated these two colonies as they had for the previous half century.

English and Welsh Baptists and Scottish and Scots-Irish Presbyterians also energetically increased their presence in the British colonies after 1690. Baptists from Wales and England emigrated to Pennsylvania and New Jersey in substantial enough numbers between 1680 and 1740 that

DUM·CLAVUM·TENEAM

William Penn Esq.ʳ Proprietor of Penſylvania 1703

The wealthy William Penn, whose coat of arms is depicted here, founded Pennsylvania as a haven for Quakers and promised religious toleration to most Christians. The Latin reads, "As long as I hold the key."

This brick hexagonal Quaker meeting house in Burlington, New Jersey, survived the Revolution, but was demolished in the 1780s to build a larger meeting house with a school.

soon they greatly outnumbered the few Baptist congregations that had emerged in New England between 1640 and 1690.

Ethnic identity defined membership in most of the Pennsylvania and New Jersey Baptist congregations. Most were Calvinists who accepted the doctrine of predestination but also reserved the rite of baptism for adults, like Baptists elsewhere. The Baptist congregation in Philadelphia contained mostly English settlers; in contrast, many rural Baptist congregations were Welsh. By 1710 more than 20 Baptist congregations existed in Pennsylvania and New Jersey, and by 1740 there were more than 60 Baptist congregations throughout the colonies from New England to Virginia and North and South Carolina.

Church government, rather than theology, separated Presbyterians from Baptists and Congregationalists. All three were Calvinist in theology, but the Presbyterians, unlike the Baptists, baptized children. Equally important, the Presbyterians stressed a hierarchical church government that the New England Congregationalists rejected. Their "presbyteries" and "synods," controlled by clergymen, exercised authority over individual congregations. Presbyteries governed congregations in several regions, and a synod supervised the presbyteries.

Presbyterians quickly outnumbered Baptists throughout the British settlements on the North American continent. Before 1690 no more than a handful of Presbyterian congregations existed in the colonies. But by 1710 almost 30 Presbyterian congregations had been formed, and by 1740 the number had reached more than 130. English settlers made up some of these congregations, especially in the cities of Boston, New York, and Charleston. In New Jersey several old Congregationalist churches founded by emigrants from New England affiliated with the Presbyterians after losing touch with their Congregationalist origins.

Most new Presbyterian congregations were filled with immigrants, however. Many were Scots-Irish—the children and grandchildren of Scottish men and women who had settled in northern Ireland in the 17th century to aid the English in their subjugation of the Irish. The Scots-Irish who moved on from Ireland to America settled throughout the colonies, from New England to North Carolina. More new Presbyterians were immigrants from Scotland itself. Not all of them had been Presbyterians at home. Late-17th- and early-18th-century Scotland contained many different religious groups, not only Presbyterians but Quakers as well as adherents of the Church of Scotland, which was allied with the Church of England. But in both Scotland and America, active missionary efforts and effective organization by the Presbyterians won many Scots over to Presbyterianism. As a result, by 1740 the misnomer *Scotch Presbyterian* (the term *Scotch* properly refers to the alcoholic drink) actually described the religious affiliation of most Scots in America (and in Scotland), although this Presbyterian identity had not been as secure a half century earlier on either side of the Atlantic.

Finally, groups old and new began to splinter in America, a process that later typified many 19th- and 20th-century U.S. religious groups.

For example, in the 1670s dissident Baptists in Rhode Island led by John Rogers established a separate religious movement called the Rogerenes. They worshiped on Saturday, not Sunday, and apparently rejected the use of medicine in healing, depending exclusively on prayer to cure diseases and heal injuries. Although they won substantial numbers of followers in their early years, the Rogerenes' strength never extended far beyond Rhode Island and eastern Connecticut, and the group declined after 1740.

Quakers led by the Scottish Quaker intellectual George Keith split the movement in Pennsylvania in the 1690s so seriously that the church's authorities in Philadelphia hauled him into court to silence him. But Keith never overcame the power of the Quaker authorities, and his followers soon divided into Keithian Quakers, then Keithian Baptists. Some returned to the Quakers, others became Baptists, and George Keith himself became a Church of England minister who toured the colonies preaching against the Quakers in the early 1700s.

The survival and surprising strength of magical practices further complicated the British American religious landscape after 1690. Historians formerly thought that most magical beliefs and practices died out in the colonies after the 1692 Salem witch trials. New studies have shown, however, that this was not necessarily true. On at least two occasions authorities held additional witch trials in the colonies after 1692. Virginia authorities tried a woman named Grace Sherwood for witchcraft in 1705 and used the so-called dunking test to prove the charge. If she floated in water, she was guilty; if she sank, she was innocent—albeit dead by drowning. Unfortunately, the court records are incomplete, and Sherwood's fate remains unknown.

In 1706 the chief justice of South Carolina, Nicholas Trott, wrote a learned treatise demanding that the Charleston grand jury prosecute witches. Trott supported his demand with quotations from many authorities advocating the prosecution of witches, including the Puritan clergyman Increase Mather. But the grand jury refused to do so and apparently called witchcraft illusory, not real. This decision dismayed one local clergyman. He worried that "the Spirit of the Devil should be so much respected as to make men call open witchcraft" merely "imagination and no more." No more attempts to prosecute witches are known in the colonial period, although rumors about witchcraft popped up in Massachusetts and Virginia in the 1720s and 1740s.

European immigration after 1690 introduced new sources of magical and occult beliefs that still circulated throughout Europe. The prominent Lutheran clergyman Henry Melchior Muhlenberg conducted a one-man crusade against magic and occultism among German immigrants in the 1740s and 1750s. He complained that Pennsylvania contained "more necromancers," or practitioners of magic, "than Christians," and that old people in Germany harbored especially "superstitious and godless notions." Yet Muhlenberg worried about Pennsylvania's younger immigrants as well: "Their heads, too, are full of fantastic notions of witchcraft and Satanic arts." In response, Muhlenberg publicly ridiculed ghost stories as "hocus-pocus" and a sin against God. When he learned that an immigrant named Simon Graf "dealt in witchcraft and exorcism of devils," he excluded Graf from his congregation until Graf "burned his books and publicly confessed his offense before the congregation." Graf repented, and at his death Muhlenberg used the story of Graf's repudiation of magic to make a "good impression upon the congregation," because it knew about Graf's former practice of magic.

"Cunning people" who found lost objects and cured diseases also remained in the colonies after 1690. A man in Tiverton, Massachusetts, cast horoscopes and reportedly located lost objects for seamen using magical means, and a woman in Newport, Rhode Island, made urine cakes for use in predicting the future. Much to his disgust, the Reverend Ebenezer Parkman reported in 1755 that after extensive searches and prayers had failed to locate a child lost in the woods near Wachusett, Massachusetts, neighbors resorted to a blacksmith and "wise man" to find the child by using magic. An astrologers' society in Pennsylvania briefly taught magical arts to inquiring students in the 1690s, and in 1723 Pennsylvania Quaker leaders renewed an earlier denunciation of wise men and women who "pretend to discover things hiddenly transacted, or tell where things lost or stolen may be found."

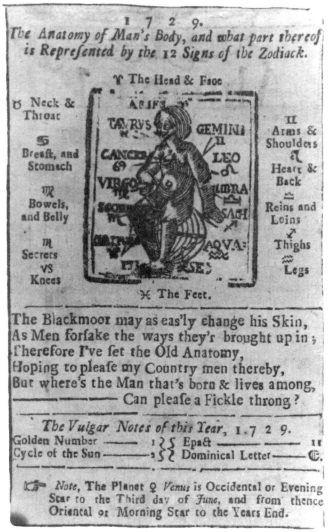

Almanacs contained the most important sources of magical and occult information available to colonists after 1690. Up to the time of the American Revolution, many almanacs included a picture called the "anatomy," a crude figure of a man circled by the signs of the zodiac—representations, that is, of the principal planets, moon, and sun, which were said to control various parts of the body. Even men and women who could barely read could use such an illustration to match occult medicines to their diseases or injuries and seek cures.

Almanac makers sometimes complained about pressure to include astrological or occult information in them. Samuel Clough's *New York Almanac* for 1703 included a poem that carped about readers' demands to see such material in every almanac:

> The anatomy must still be in,
> Else the almanac's not worth a pin,
> For country-men regard the sign,
> As though it were oracle divine.

Although these magical beliefs survived in the 18th-century colonies, they certainly declined among the educated elite. The president of Yale, Ezra Stiles, admitted in the 1780s that magic "subsists among some almanac makers and fortune tellers." But he believed that "in general the system is broken up, the vessel of sorcery shipwrecked, and only some scattered planks and pieces disjoined floating and scattered on the ocean of…human activity and bustle." Still, even its remnants increased the already spectacular religious diversity of 18th-century colonial America.

Astrological beliefs persisted throughout the 18th-century British colonies. Nathaniel Ames's 1729 *Almanac* included the "anatomy" that showed the different parts of the body controlled by various signs of the zodiac.

Not everyone responded positively to colonial religious diversity. Many settlers found such religious variety puzzling, or even disturbing. This was well demonstrated in the experience of Charles Woodmason, a Church of England minister who preached in the backcountry of North Carolina in the 1760s. Most of Woodmason's listeners belonged to no church, although they heard many different preachers. They were rough and untutored. Woodmason had to remind them how to behave in church: "Bring no dogs with you. They are very troublesome.... When you are seated, do not whisper, talk, [or] gaze about .... If you are thirsty, pray drink before you enter."

But often, Woodmason's listeners simply did not know what to make of the religious choices swirling around them. Nothing in Europe had prepared them for it, and the results were not always attractive, at least not in Woodmason's mind. He wrote in his journal after a visit to Lynch's Creek, North Carolina, in 1767, that the residents "complained of being eaten up by itinerant teachers, preachers, and impostors...Baptists, New Lights, Presbyterians, Independents, and a hundred other sects, so that one day you might hear this system of doctrine, the next day another." People were so confused that they simply could not choose. Woodmason described the result succinctly: "By the variety of tailors who would pretend to know [how]...Christ's coat is to be worn, none will put it on." Many colonists enjoyed the religious freedom that had emerged in America. But not everyone grappled easily with the confusion it produced.

Chapter 4

African and American Indian Religion

n the mid-1600s Mohegans living in eastern Connecticut interred several bodies at their principal burial ground, near modern-day Norwich. Along with the body of Lucy Occum, who had been converted to Christianity yet was also a medicine woman, the Mohegans had placed a bowl inlaid with wampum, the brightly colored cylindrical beads often used as currency in Indian transactions. With Hannah Wequot, the daughter of Chief Uncas, a 17th-century Mohegan leader, they had buried a bowl carved from a pepperidge tree knot and decorated with the figure of an owl. With a third, unknown Mohegan they had included a small "Hobbomocko" doll used to ward off evil spirits.

In 1868 looters invaded the Mohegan burial mound, scattering skeletons and removing hundreds of items buried with them, including the Hobbomocko doll and the bowls buried with Lucy Occum and Hannah Uncas. The looters sold most of the items they retrieved to collectors, and some later found their way to museums. In 1990, however, Congress passed the Native American Graves Protection and Repatriation Act, which required museums to return burial objects to the surviving tribes for reburial. This act honored a spiritual reality crucial to Native American life, that burial objects, like the dead themselves, carried immense religious meaning. Such relics were not art for homes and museums but spiritual objects that were to accompany the dead in new lives and jour-

Absalom Jones, a former slave, was a founder of the Free African Society in Philadelphia, one of the first two African-American Methodist churches formed in America.

neys. Since the passage of the law in 1990 thousands of items, ranging from sacred objects to skeletons, have been returned to their original sources and reburied. Yale University's Peabody Museum, which acquired the three Mohegan objects through purchase in the early 20th century, returned them to the Mohegan nation in 1998, and they were reburied at the Royal Mohegan burial ground 350 years after they had been placed there, some 130 years after their theft.

In the 1990s a remarkably different kind of exhumation cast new light on African-American religious life in New York City between 1690 and 1794. In 1991 archaeologists examining ground in lower Manhattan prior to the construction of a $276 million federal office building unexpectedly uncovered more than 400 graves of African Americans. The site was later determined to have been the "Negro Burial Ground" used from the 1690s until its closure in 1794, then later forgotten when graveyard markers were obliterated and buildings were constructed on the site.

Analysis of this site, together with additional archaeological evidence from other African burial sites on the eastern seaboard, provides important clues to understanding African-American religious practices in the colonial era. Skeletons often bespoke the horrific conditions of New World slavery. Many of these, which were of children, were in numbers that suggested the difficulties that African Americans faced in sustaining family life in the colonial era. The remains of adults frequently showed broken bones, most likely sustained in work or from punishment.

The archaeological evidence also suggests that African Americans tried to follow traditional Old World African burial customs in the colonial settlements. The New York authorities, among others, did not make this easy. By law, no more than a dozen African Americans were allowed to attend a slave funeral, and coffins could not be covered, for fear that slaves would conceal weapons under the pall. Yet as early as the 1710s a Church of England minister acknowledged that most New York slaves were buried without Christian services and that "heathenish rites are performed over them." What these rites were is impossible now to say. But beads, shells, and polished stones often accompanied the remains found in the New York burial site and in 18th-century African-American burials in Virginia and Maryland. They suggest that traditional African religious customs persisted in the face of obstacles that were quite unknown to the adherents of European religions.

The story of Native American religion during the British colonial period is simultaneously a tale of disappearance, change, and resilience. Enormous numbers of Native American religions simply disappeared, because so many of the cultures and societies that sustained them became extinct. Native American religions also often changed, sometimes adopting and adapting to Christianity, at others taking on new elements that also honored traditional concerns. As Native American cultures evolved, the Indians often found new ways to express old ideas and develop new ones, processes that also have been central to Christianity and Judaism throughout their engagement with Western civilization.

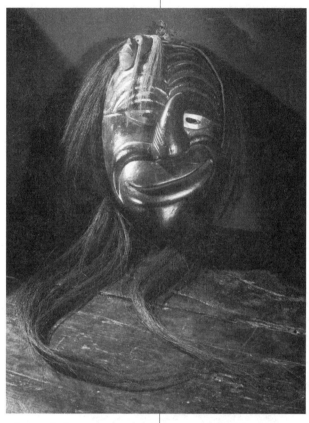

Eighteenth-century Iroquois shamans used False Face masks in healing ceremonies to mollify or frighten malicious spirits.

The outright disappearance of many distinctive Indian societies, and of the religions that sustained them, constitutes one of the most distressing facts of early American religious history. Between 100 and 200 Indian societies disappeared by the time of the American Revolution, and more became extinct in the 19th century. Most fell victim to devastating diseases, like cholera and smallpox, that had been introduced by Europeans, and the small size of many Indian societies, sometimes as few as 500 or 1,000 people, made disease among them unusually devastating. In the southeastern United States alone, groups that became extinct included the Chilucan and Oconee of Florida; the Tacatacuru, Yufera, and Yui of Georgia; the Chawasha of Mississippi; the Cape Fear and Chowanoc of

North Carolina; the Sewee, Shakori, and Waxhaw of South Carolina; and the Manahoac, Monacan, Moneton, Nahyssan, and Occaneechi of Virginia. Some, like the Ais, Guacata, and Jeaga Indians of Florida, fled to Cuba, probably about 1763, at the end of the French and Indian War, where they were absorbed into the native population. As these cultures disappeared, so too did their religions.

The Indians who survived responded in a variety of ways to Christian missionary endeavors. The efforts at conversion in Virginia brought few results. The early Virginians proved more adept at attacking Indians than at converting them. The early missionary efforts by the first ministers in Virginia quickly evaporated, and most Indians rejected the Christian gospel even when it was offered. An Indian uprising in 1622, which resulted in 300 deaths among the English settlers—almost a quarter of the colony's population—brought an end to the missionary efforts and turned the English toward even more aggressive expansion. The Virginians fought a major war against the Indians in 1676 that reduced the colony's Indian population to less than 1,000.

The Native American who welcomed Puritans on the seal of the Massachusetts Bay Company was a better representation of the Puritans' hopes than of actual Indian sentiment.

The seal of the Massachusetts Bay Company, which held the charter to the colony of Massachusetts, featured an Indian carrying a bow and arrow standing between two pine trees and saying, "Come over and help us." The Puritans' missionary efforts among the Indians, unlike the Virginians', achieved some success. The Puritan minister John Eliot spent his entire career in Massachusetts seeking conversions among the Indians. The Puritans published more than 20 religious books in the Massachusett language between 1654 and 1690, including a complete translation of the Bible, with enough copies printed to distribute one to every 2.5 Indians. Converted Indians themselves preached among other Indians. By 1674 more than 30 so-called "praying towns" of

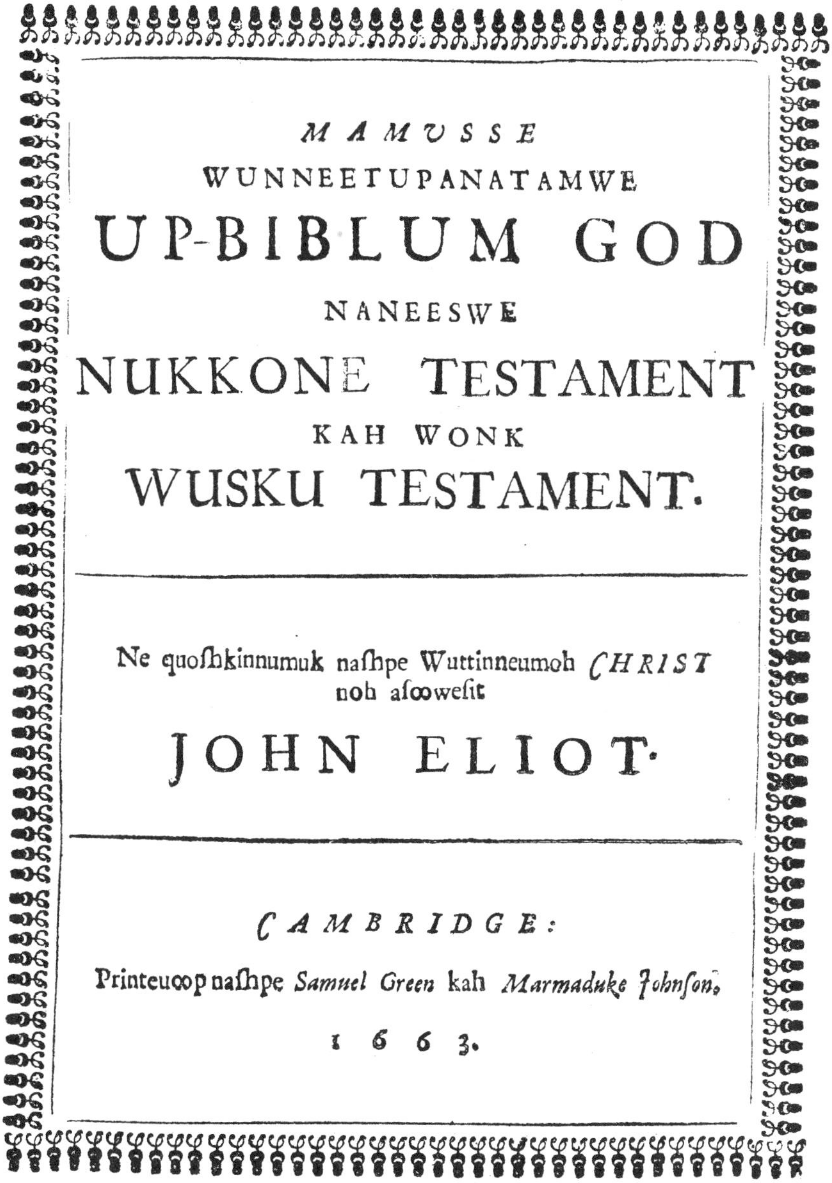

MAMUSSE

WUNNEETUPANATAMWE

UP-BIBLUM GOD

NANEESWE

NUKKONE TESTAMENT

KAH WONK

WUSKU TESTAMENT.

Ne quoſhkinnumuk naſhpe Wuttinneumoh *CHRIST*
noh aſꝏweſit

JOHN ELIOT·

CAMBRIDGE:

Printeuꝏp naſhpe *Samuel Green* kah *Marmaduke Johnſon,*

1 6 6 3.

John Eliot published his Massachusett translation of the New Testament in 1663. More of the books probably were given to Eliot's English supporters than to Indians.

Christian Indians dotted Massachusetts. All told, about 1,600 Christian Indians lived on the mainland and on Martha's Vineyard.

Yet the Puritan success was not what it seemed. Few Indians could read Eliot's translated Bibles because like many Puritans themselves, Indians seldom learned to read. Indeed, Eliot's Bibles may have been

Paul Revere engraved this imagined portrait of the Indian leader Metacom, called King Philip by the English. The picture appeared in the 1772 edition of Benjamin Church's first-hand account of King Philip's War of 1676, in which Church described Metacom's capture, execution, and gruesome quartering.

published mainly for English promoters of Indian missionary work. Fewer than 20 percent of the Indians in the "praying towns" received Christian baptism, and the Massachusett leader Metacom, known to the English as Philip, never converted to Christianity. Eliot demanded that the Indians abandon their traditional Indian religion completely, including its age-old medical customs and reliance upon the shamans, or medicine men and women, who practiced it. At the same time, the English settlers and the Indians squabbled frequently about property rights and English expansion into formerly Indian territory.

The so-called King Philip's War of 1675–76 effectively ended Eliot's work. In 1675 Indians led by Metacom attacked English settlements. They devastated 25 English villages, destroyed more than 1,000 English homes, and killed at least 2,000 English men and women and 8,000 cattle. The English counterattacked vengefully, killing Metacom and upward of 7,000 Indians, some in battle, others by starvation and disease. They reduced the "praying towns" to four, several of which quickly disbanded. They sold many Indians as slaves in the West Indies and put others out as servants in Massachusetts. If the war ended the Indian threat to New England, it also stopped any extensive effort at establishing Puritan Indian missions for decades. Many Indians were dead or gone, English sympathies for setting up missions evaporated, and John Eliot, now more than 70 years old, was too frail to carry on.

By comparison, the Jesuits who brought Catholicism to the Indians in Canada proved substantially more successful. The Jesuits worked more patiently and learned more about native customs and life, not just the native language. They introduced Christian physical objects like rosaries, crucifixes, and rings that superficially resembled physical objects used in Indian worship like medicine clubs and sticks. They offered richly appointed altars with burning candles. Catholic visual images helped strengthen the Indians' regard for Christianity. The Jesuits refrained from explaining the concept behind the sacrament of Christian communion, in which bread and wine are believed to be transformed into Christ's body and blood, fearing that it would be thought of as cannibalism, and described it instead as a commemorative service.

Even more than the Puritans, the Jesuits were superb logicians whose understanding of the Indian way of life made them better able to refute Indian objections to Christianity. Most importantly, as one Jesuit put it himself, to win converts they used "mildness and force, threats and prayers, labors and tears." They understood that conversion was an emotional as well as a logical process. As one Jesuit put it, "In order to convert these peoples, one must begin by touching their hearts, before he can convince their minds."

The Jesuits met with considerable success among the Hurons in southern Canada and northern New York. By 1648 they counted 22 Jesuits working in numerous Huron villages with almost 50 native assistants. But

These illustrations in Father Chrestien Le Clerq's *Nouvelle Relation de la Gaspésie* (A New Account of the Gaspesie) showed European readers how Jesuit missionaries taught Indians to pray and worship.

an unexpected attack from the Iroquois had murderous effects on the Hurons and brought much Jesuit work to a stop. The Iroquois killed thousands of Hurons, destroyed many of their villages, and killed the principal Jesuit missionary to the Hurons, Jean de Brébeuf. The Iroquois were so impressed with Brébeuf's bravery that they ate his heart and drank his blood to absorb his strength. The Jesuits retained the allegiance of the remaining Hurons, and thousands more Hurons underwent Christian baptism after the Iroquois war ended. But the Huron nation remained a pale reflection of its former self after the Iroquois attacks, and the Jesuits' missionary efforts toward them suffered with it.

More denominations became involved in missions to the Indians in the 18th-century British colonies, though not always with great success. The Church of England sponsored a mere handful of missions among the Indians and succeeded with even fewer. The Congregationalist minister Eleazar Wheelock trained Indians at a special school in Lebanon, Connecticut, and later at what would become Dartmouth College, in New Hampshire. He separated Indian students from their native communities so he could train and discipline them without interference. Samson Occom, a Mohegan, who became Wheelock's greatest success story, ministered to the Indians in Long Island, New England, and New York City. But Wheelock and Occom won relatively few converts, and Wheelock's school was generally considered a failure.

Moravian missionaries in New York and Pennsylvania experienced greater success. Like the Jesuits, the Moravians made a point of learning much about the native cultures and exhibited considerable patience in awaiting conversions. They also distanced themselves from aggressive government policies on English settlement and warfare. But most importantly, Moravian theology fit the realities of the conversion process and important themes in traditional native beliefs. The Moravians stressed piety and the love of Christ, both of which could be learned by example. Unlike the Puritans, they did not stress doctrine. The Moravians lived among the Indians and used native language in day-to-day conversation, not merely in translated books. Like the Native Americans, they discussed

how dreams could communicate religious truths and moral lessons. A Presbyterian observer in Pennsylvania commented enviously, "The Moravians appear to have adopted the best mode of Christianizing the Indians. They go among them without noise or parade, and by their friendly behavior conciliate their good will."

Few Indians ever converted to Christianity, yet there was substantial change throughout the Indian religious world during the British colonial era. This was not surprising. Just as Christianity changed drastically after it became the official religion of the Roman Empire, the native religions of North America changed greatly as contact with Europeans drastically altered native cultures. The changes in nature and ecology produced by European colonization greatly threatened many native religions. The extraordinary slaughtering of animals that came in with the Europeans undermined the beliefs that assigned crucial supernatural roles to animals, for example. The Micmacs of far eastern Canada found their special relationship with the beaver imperiled by unchecked harvesting of beaver skins, a trade the Micmacs themselves indulged. The spirits residing in nature no longer spoke. Later, in the mid-18th century, the Micmacs tore out the eyes of beavers and other animals they killed as a way of blinding the animals to the treatment the animals were now receiving.

Other Indian groups demonstrated remarkable resilience in the face of multiple threats to their political, cultural, and spiritual universe. One form this took was to incorporate the material goods that the Europeans brought into their own existing religious milieu. This "syncretism," or fusing of different beliefs and cultures, stimulated the survival of native

These animals constituted some of the totems, or family or clan emblems, adopted by native American groups in 18th-century New York.

cultures and beliefs and demonstrated the creative adaptability of native cultures and religions. A Micmac medicine woman used Catholic rosary beads as the centerpiece of her Micmac healing practice. As an unhappy Jesuit priest described it, "These she carefully preserved, and gave them only to those who were her friends, protesting...that the gift which she gave them had come originally from heaven."

New cultures and new religious systems emerged among the Indians as European expansion continued. A new "Catawba" nation emerged between 1700 and 1740 from an array of endangered separate peoples in North and South Carolina, among them the Eno, Cape Fear, Cheraw, Congaree, Cusago, Keyauwee, Santee, Saponi, Sissipahaw, Sugeree, Waccamaw, Wateree, Winyaw, and Woccon Indians. The new Catawba culture created a new Indian society. Its religious expressions mixed elements from the older Indian societies as well as Christianity, which some Indians had learned through missionaries. One Catawba, a former Saponi Indian named Ned Bearskin, described for the Virginia planter William Byrd the Catawba belief in a single supreme being who punished goodness and badness.

This was not, however, the Christian God of a Christian world. Bearskin described a sacred world where deer and turkey meat could not be mixed, where the "regions of bliss" after death contained beautiful women and men, abundant game, and plentiful crops, and where "regions of misery" brought cold, hunger, and constant sexual aggressiveness. New ceremonies bound Catawbas together in life and death. Their rituals commemorated harvests and honored the dead. In shaping these new spiritual expressions the Catawbas, like other Native Americans, wrested meaning from endangerment and cleared the way for survival into modern times.

African religions also experienced exceptional difficulties under British slavery that were at least as severe as those experienced by American Indian religions and far beyond any difficulties known to Christianity and Judaism. Ultimately, no African religions survived whole in the British colonies of North America. Thus, the religions from the Ashanti or Ibo societies on Africa's west coast, for example, were no longer practiced on the North American continent in the broad, expansive fashion they had been observed in Africa. This made the story of African religions in British America remarkably different from the history of all the other immigrant religions in America. No other Old World peoples suffered such wholesale destruction of their traditional religions as did Africans enslaved in Britain's North American colonies. Yet despite the odds against them, Africans reconstructed in America some key elements of their traditional religious practice and slowly reconfigured Christianity according to their own needs; in the process, they would leave their imprint upon the wider Christian world.

The destruction of the traditional African religious systems in the British colonies stemmed from two primary causes: the religious havoc caused by capture and New World enslavement, and the repressiveness of British slavery. The African slave trade disregarded the individual slaves' spirituality. Slave traders were interested in workers, not spiritual leaders. Africans who exercised special religious leadership in their home societies arrived in America only by accident, not intent. Worse, the variety of African religions reduced the spiritual guidance one person might give to many captured Africans. The Akan, Ashanti, Dahoman, Ibo, and Yoruba societies were as religiously and culturally distinct as were the Scottish, Welsh, English, French, and Spanish societies of Europe. As a result, a religious figure from one African society would have found it difficult to provide spiritual leadership for the many enslaved Africans from other societies.

Slaveholders in America suppressed public African religious practice in almost all areas except burials and, possibly, marriages or betrothals. Planters, farmers, and merchants who owned slaves worried most about Africans' use of religious meetings as places to hatch resistance and rebellion and actively opposed African religious gatherings. An Anglican min-

This Asante drum, found in Virginia in the colonial period, was made of wood from Africa. It probably had been carried to America aboard a slave ship.

A Christian Missionary Learns about Native Americans' Religion

The Reverend David Brainerd, a Presbyterian missionary to Native Americans in New Jersey and Pennsylvania in the 1740s, was fascinated by their religion. Brainerd wrote that they were "brutishly stupid and ignorant of divine things" and "obstinately set against Christianity." But Brainerd also recorded traditional Indian religious beliefs with surprising sensitivity in a report he published in Philadelphia in 1746, Mirabilia Dei inter Indicos; or, The Rise and Progress of a Remarkable Work of Grace Amongst a Number of the Indians in the Provinces of New-Jersey and Pennsylvania.

I have taken much pains to inquire of my Christian people [Indians converted to Christianity], whether they, before their acquaintance with Christianity, imagined there was a plurality of great invisible powers....So far as I can learn, they had a notion of a plurality of indivisible deities, and paid some kind of homage to them promiscuously, under a great variety of forms and shapes. And it is certain, those who yet remain Pagans pay some kind of superstitious reverence to beasts, birds, fishes, and even reptiles; that is, some to one kind of animal, and some to another. They do not indeed suppose a divine power essential to, or inhering in these creatures, but that some indivisible beings...communicate to these animals a great power, either one or other of them, or perhaps sometimes all of them, and so make these creatures the immediate authors of good to certain persons.

They seem to have some confused notion about a future state of existence, and many of them imagine that the *chichung,* (i.e., the shadow), or what survives the body, will at death go southward, and in an unknown but curious place, will enjoy some kind of happiness, such as, hunting, feasting, dancing, and the like....I remember I once consulted a very ancient, but intelligent Indian upon this point, for my own satisfaction; asked him whether the Indians of old times had supposed there was anything of the man that would survive the body? He replied, Yes. I asked him, where they supposed its abode would be? He replied, "It would go southward." I asked him further, whether it would be happy there? He answered, after a considerable pause, "that the souls of good folks would be happy, and the souls of bad folks miserable." I then asked him, who he called bad folks? His answer (as I remember) was, "Those who lie, steal, quarrel with their neighbors, are unkind to their friends, and especially to aged parents, and, in a word, such as are a plague to mankind."

They give much heed to dreams, because they suppose these invisible powers give them directions at such times about certain affairs, and sometime inform them what animal they would chuse to be worshipped in. They are likewise much attached to the traditions and fabulous notions of their fathers, who have informed them of diverse miracles that were anciently wrought among the Indians, which they firmly believe, and thence look upon their ancestors to have been the best of men.

ister in South Carolina acknowledged that he readily suppressed African "feasts, dances, and merry meetings upon the Lord's day." The laws in most colonies prohibited meetings of Africans for any reason. Finally, since large-scale slaveholding in America was rare, most enslaved Africans lived in small groups on small farms widely separated from other Africans. These conditions made the public and collective practice of traditional African religion extraordinarily difficult in America.

English efforts to convert slaves to Christianity met with little success before the American Revolution. In fact, many slaveholders actively resisted attempts to convert the Africans. They worried that Christian baptism would undermine the concept of enslavement and encourage Africans to regard themselves as the equals of their owners. One South Carolina slaveholder told his minister that he would "never come to the [communion] table while slaves are received." Another asked, "If any of my slaves go to heaven…must I see them there?" The Reverend Francis Le Jau tried to appease his South Carolina parishioners by forcing slaves to take an oath that they did not seek baptism "out of any design to free yourself from the duty and obedience you owe to your master while you live." The effort satisfied few owners, and most slaves remained unbaptized.

Between 1690 and 1750 few Africans converted to Christianity. Anglicans conducted most of the occasional efforts at slave conversion before 1750. They operated schools for slaves in New York City in the early decades of the 18th century, but they never produced large numbers of converts. Rural Anglican clergymen ministering where most Africans lived reported few converts there, and most eventually abandoned serious work among Africans. Presbyterians preached to enslaved Africans in Virginia and North Carolina in the 1750s and 1760s but won few converts. The Presbyterian minister Samuel Davies preached among Africans but denied baptism to them because he worried, like Le Jau, that they sought an "equality with their masters."

In contrast, several specific African rites did survive capture and enslavement despite the harshness of British slaveholding. South Carolina planters complained about "rites and revels" carried out among recently

arrived Africans. Some owners recognized the validity of marriages among Africans that were not sanctioned by colonial law or by other owners. More importantly, Africans recognized these marriages among themselves and gathered to celebrate them. A rare 18th-century picture, probably from South Carolina, most likely depicts one of these marriage celebrations. The slave owner's home is in the far background, only Africans are depicted, the musical instruments are African, and the dancing suggests the joy of a major occasion, such as a marriage, perhaps of the woman seated to the left and the man in the white coat kneeling next to her.

Africans also consulted conjurers who invoked traditional African magic and medical knowledge to cure disease and harm enemies, whether slaves or owners. An African "sorcerer" reputedly supplied magical powder to shield Africans from European weapons before launching a bloody but unsuccessful revolt in New York City in 1712. Two Africans won

Black and white Moravians worship together in Johann Valentin Haidt's 1747 painting *Erstlingsbild (The First Fruits)*. **The unique success of Moravian proselytizing among West Indian slaves contrasted sharply with English Protestant failures in converting mainland colonial Africans.**

In 1781, Thomas Jefferson noted that "The instrument proper to the [slaves] is the Banjar, which they brought hither from Africa." Over time this instrument would develop into the present-day banjo.

public recognition from whites for cures, a Virginian whose medicine reputedly healed "the Yawes, Lame Distemper, Pox, Dropsy etc." and a South Carolinian who discovered a cure for rattlesnake bites. Both were most likely African "conjure men" who possessed formidable knowledge of herbs, plants, and African magical lore. At least one South Carolina poisoning case offered evidence that the African perpetrator had obtained poison from a conjurer and that several victims had employed other conjurers to ward off the poison.

Funeral rites among slaves sometimes employed African burial rituals. Slave owners appear to have been more tolerant of at least some African ceremonies at death than of other African religious practices. Several African burial sites from 18th-century Maryland contain corpses buried with beads, bracelets, wreaths, and large numbers of seeds. The Africans interred in one Maryland site lacked clothing or shrouds, as though the dead were to be born again in a new life. It is unclear, however, whether Africans were left to bury their fellows as they saw fit; it may be that they performed rites of their own following a Christian ceremony. A Scots traveler in North Carolina reported in 1774 that after the Christian funeral of an African woman "the Negroes assembled to perform their part of the funeral rites, which they did by running, jumping, crying and various exercises."

After 1760 enslaved Africans were exposed to new missionary efforts by Baptists and Methodists. These efforts led to the founding of the many African-American Christian churches that flowered in the 19th century. The Baptist and Methodist preaching among Africans that developed in the 1760s and 1770s differed considerably from earlier Anglican and Presbyterian efforts at Christian conversion. The Anglicans and Presbyterians stressed ritual and doctrine, not experience. The Anglicans never accorded Africans congregational membership, and the Presbyterians often refused to baptize Africans. The Anglican revivalist George Whitefield evangelized among enslaved Africans and criticized slaveholders in his first trip to America in 1739 and 1740. But Whitefield also accepted slavery, and regularly purchased slaves to work on the plantation that he had begun for orphans in Bethesda, Georgia, in the 1740s.

In contrast, evangelical Baptists and Methodists stressed the conversion experience and encouraged shouting, trembling, and ecstatic singing in their services. They often promoted millennialist beliefs that Christ would return to earth for a 1,000-year reign and emphasized the transformation of personal life that came with Christian conversion. They evangelized among poorer whites and quickly began preaching among enslaved Africans as well. By the early 1770s both the Baptists and the Methodists had baptized hundreds of Africans, in the southern colonies especially. Most importantly, some Baptist preachers, such as Elhanan Winchester, openly condemned slavery and slaveholding.

Africans who became Baptists and Methodists quickly exercised a religious leadership unknown among either the Anglicans or Presbyterians. Africans often became members of Baptist congregations, and some

The African poet Phillis Wheatley of Boston embraced evangelical Christianity and at the age of 14 wrote "An Address to the Atheist."

An Address to the Atheist. By P Wheatley at the age of
14 years. — 1767.

Muse! where shall I begin the spacious feild
To tell what curses unbeleif doth yeild?
Thou who dost daily feel his hand, and rod
Darest thou deny the Essence of a God!
If there's no heav'n, ah! whither wilt thou go
Make thy Elysium in the shades below?
If there's no God from whom did all things spring
He made the greatest and minutest Thing
Angelic ranks no less his power display
Than the least mite scarce visible to Day
With vast astonishment my Soul is struck
Have Reason's powers thy dark breast forsook?
The Laws deep graven by the hand of God,
Seal'd with Immanuels' all-redeeming blood:
This second point thy folly dares deny
On thy devoted head for vengeance cry —
Turn then I pray thee from the dangerous road
Rise from the dust and seek the mighty God.
His is bright truth without a dark disguise
And his are wisdom's all beholding Eyes.
With labour'd snares our Adversary great
With holds from us the Kingdom and the seat
Bliss weeping waits thee, in her Arms to fly
To her own regions of felicity —
Perhaps thy ignorance will ask us where?
Go to the Corner stone he will declare.
Thy heart in unbeleif will harden'd grow
Tho' much indulg'd in vicious pleasure now —
Thou tak'st unusual means; the path forbear
Unkind to others to thy self severe
Methinks I see the consequence thou'rt blind
Thy unbeleif disturbs the peaceful Mind.

African Baptists began preaching, at least to fellow Africans. George Liele, born into slavery in Virginia to a master who was himself a convert to the Baptist movement, began preaching to his fellow slaves in the 1770s. After Liele was freed by his master in 1777 he moved to Savannah, Georgia, where he founded the town's first separate African Baptist congregation, the First African Church of Savannah.

Enslaved and free Africans alike quickly became prominent in the early Methodist movement. The Methodists evangelized heavily in the British West Indies among enslaved Africans, and in the southern colonies they won converts among both the poorer whites and enslaved Africans. Methodist itinerant preachers such as Freeborn Garrettson freely described Maryland Methodist gatherings as racially mixed: "I suppose about twelve whites and blacks were present. The power of the Lord came among us." Sometimes the power or the message or the preacher proved dangerous for the Methodists, however. David Margate, an African trained by Methodists in England, preached to slaves in South Carolina in 1775. But when he claimed that he was a second Moses and had been "called to

Rev. Lemuel Haynes, an African-American Congregationalist clergyman, ministered to white congregations in Connecticut and Vermont between the 1790s and his death in 1833.

deliver his people from slavery," the Methodist authorities returned him to England, fearful of his rhetoric and intentions.

The Revolution interrupted these developments, if only for a moment. When it ended, the example of African preaching among Baptists and Methodists created new opportunities and, eventually, new religious movements for enslaved and free Africans in America. After the Revolution, African Baptist preachers worked regularly from Pennsylvania to South Carolina. A Williamsburg, Virginia, court tried to stop the preaching of an African Baptist named Moses because he drew such large crowds. Another African Baptist, Gowan Pamphlet, formed a separate African Baptist congregation in Williamsburg that was admitted to the local white Baptist association in 1791. By 1800, at least a dozen independent African Baptist congregations existed in the United States, most of them formed by free or enslaved African preachers.

Africans also claimed important places within the post-Revolutionary Methodist movement. "Black Harry Hosier" preached regularly with Methodist leaders Francis Asbury, Thomas Coke, and Freeborn Garrettson despite white objections to his race. Other African Methodist preachers campaigned in Virginia and Maryland. Sometimes tensions resulted when Africans followed African preachers. On one occasion a white Methodist who was preaching to a racially mixed congregation lost his African listeners when an African Methodist preacher joined him. When the African began preaching, the African listeners "immediately flocked around, while I myself could be suffered to preach and pray in the church." In Philadelphia, free Africans who had previously worshiped with whites formed two congregations of their own in 1794. One, led by an African American named Absalom Jones, was first called simply the African Church but was later renamed St. Thomas's. The other, led by Richard Allen, emerged from within the Methodist movement and was later called Bethel African Methodist Episcopal Church.

The African preaching among Methodists and Baptists in the late colonial era laid a foundation for post-Revolutionary religious activism among both enslaved and free Africans and for the great African-American

Christian denominations formed in the 19th century. After 1810 the Baptists created a substantial bloc of independent African congregations up and down the East Coast and in the American West. The Methodists formed two important denominations, the African Methodist Episcopal Church, organized in 1816, and the African Methodist Episcopal Zion Church, founded in 1821.

Folk religious customs drawn from a variety of African traditions in the colonial era also blossomed in the 19th century. In the early-19th-century South the tradition of "conjurers" and African medicine men and women occasionally glimpsed in the British colonies emerged into the widespread appearance of "Obeah men," a common African name for sorcerers who were consulted by both blacks and whites in the South. Indeed, even in the early 20th century the tradition still could be seen in New York City's Harlem, where a variety of "African medicine men," "herb doctors," and "spiritualists" healed and cured among the African-American population.

Despite important differences, then, the religious experiences of American Indians and Africans bore striking similarities in the colonial period. Unlike European immigrants to America, Indians and Africans faced immense difficulties continuing or extending their traditional religious practices in settings that European colonization made new for everyone. Indians and Africans employed religion in new and vital ways in colonial America. They shaped meaning and sustained community life across two extraordinarily difficult centuries, and the new religious expressions they created became central to Indian and African-American identity in the centuries that followed.

Chapter 5

Reviving Colonial Religion

n "Rip Van Winkle," Washington Irving's 1819 short story, Rip awakens from a 20-year sleep to find himself a stranger to almost everything he had known. The story contains nothing about religion. But if it did, and if Rip had slept 90 years starting in 1680, his astonishment would have been even greater. Upon awakening in 1770, he would have discovered that America was now awash in extraordinary religious pluralism; but he might have been even more startled by how religious activity itself had changed in crucial ways. All the religious denominations, old and new, formed more congregations and constructed far more church buildings in those years than they ever had in the 17th century. Revivalism, an intense campaign for religious renewal, changed the style of colonial religion. And women became increasingly prominent in colonial religious activity, even if men still exercised the authority in most religious groups. These changes, made hand in hand with the growth of religious pluralism, gave colonial religion much of the flavor characterizing it as uinquely American.

So many new congregations constructed so many new church buildings between 1680 and 1770 that they completely altered the colonial religious landscape as the American Revolution approached. More than 85 percent of the approximately 1,200 religious congregations in the colonies on the eve of the Revolution were founded after 1680. As a result, only a tiny portion of the Revolutionary-era congregations could trace their origins to the 17th century.

In the 1770s Faith Robinson Trumbull made this beautiful needlework depicting the Biblical story of the hanging of Absalom, who rebelled against his capricious father King David.

The expansion of colonial congregations occurred in two separate bursts, each with its own characteristics. The first occurred between 1680 and 1710. In this period both the New England Puritans, by then generally called Congregationalists, and the Church of England considerably expanded and strengthened their hold on important portions of the population. In New England, the Congregationalists established at least 60 new congregations between 1680 and 1710. Many of them served new towns established when younger New Englanders migrated to these settlements and as further immigrants continued to arrive from England. These new congregations carried forth New England's "state church" tradition into the 18th century in that they all received tax monies for their support. This financial support helped forestall the formation of competing congregations. A Baptist, for example, would have to pay taxes to support the legally established Congregational church in town, then also contribute to the Baptist congregation he or she might want to join.

The Church of England, the state church of that country, expanded dramatically between 1680 and 1710 throughout Britain's North American colonies. The Anglicans accomplished this feat in two ways. They strengthened the weak laws that had originally established the Church of England as the government-supported church in Virginia, and they won the legal establishment of new churches in South Carolina, North Carolina, and Maryland. As a result, all four colonies witnessed the creation of dozens of new Anglican parishes in the two decades after 1680.

In addition, Anglicans in England created the Society for the Propagation of the Gospel in Foreign Parts (SPG). The SPG raised money to support the Church of England in colonies where it lacked a legal basis and to support newly formed Anglican parishes in colonies where the Church of England was legally established. The SPG provided these churches ministers, salaries, and books, and sometimes helped construct buildings for them.

The results of both efforts were impressive. The Anglicans established almost 90 congregations in the colonies between 1680 and 1710 alone. In Maryland, which was notorious for its lack of public Christian worship before 1680, Anglicans established nearly 30 working parishes by 1710, almost all with new church buildings, two-thirds of them being staffed with resident clergymen.

A second great burst of congregational expansion occurred between 1740 and 1770. Some of it resulted from revivalism that appeared sporadically in the colonies from New England to South Carolina in this period. Eighteenth-century colonial revivalism typically stressed a "new birth" in Christ and encouraged believers to purify their lives and rejuvenate their congregations. Activist ministers led revivals in their own congregations and traveled through the countryside, preaching in friendly congregations or in the open air where local ministers opposed their work. The revivalist ministers insisted that listeners acknowledge their own depravity and seek safety in Christ. Listeners sometimes responded emotionally, occasionally shrieking and fainting when their feelings of sinfulness overcame them. The Congregationalists, Presbyterians, and Baptists benefited most from this revivalism, although a third or more of the congregations established through revivalism survived for less than a decade.

Revivalists such as George Whitefield used collapsible field pulpits when they preached out of doors in both England and America.

However, most congregations formed in the 18th century stemmed from efforts to expand religious denominations that did not necessarily support revivalism. The SPG, for example, established nearly 150 Anglican congregations throughout the colonies between 1740 and 1770. At least 400 Presbyterian and Baptist congregations were formed in this period, only some of them through revivalism. When added to the congregations formed by the Quakers, German Lutherans, German Reformed, and the Mennonites and Moravians, the era from 1740 to 1770 emerged as the single most fruitful era of congregational expansion in the entire colonial period.

After 1680 many denominations formed annual meetings, or administrative councils, to supervise church affairs in the colonies, most of them modeled on Old World institutions. Many were located in Philadelphia, which became the informal capital of colonial American Protestantism for decades. The Quakers' Philadelphia Yearly Meeting, which was modeled on the London Yearly Meeting, first met in 1685, three years after the Quaker settlement of Pennsylvania. The prominence of its leaders and the Quakers' dominance of early Pennsylvania quickly made it the most important Quaker meeting in the colonies.

The Presbytery of Philadelphia, a meeting of Presbyterian ministers and some lay elders modeled on presbyteries in Scotland and northern Ireland, first met in 1706 to supervise the Presbyterian congregations multiplying rapidly between New York and Maryland. In 1716 the Presbyterians added further regional presbyteries and created the Synod of Philadelphia to supervise the new presbyteries. By 1740 the synod had six regional presbyteries and more than 50 ministers and 70 congregations.

In 1707 the Baptists formally organized the Philadelphia Baptist Association, led by Baptists with ministerial responsibilities. It superseded the informal meetings that had been held among Baptist congregations in Pennsylvania and New Jersey since the 1680s. In 1747 German Reformed ministers established a Coetus, or assembly of ministers, in Philadelphia to manage affairs among the German Calvinists, and in 1748 German Lutherans established the Lutheran Ministerium of Pennsylvania to guide Lutheran congregational life in that colony and Maryland.

Ironically, the Church of England remained the only European religious group failing to transfer its traditional form of church government to the colonies. Political infighting in England prevented naming a bishop to supervise Anglican affairs in America. Dissenters like the Congregationalists and the Baptists feared that an Anglican bishop in America would have too much political power, and other Anglican bishops and leaders in England worried about competition from the new bishop. In the wake of this failure, Anglican officials had to depend upon ineffective "commissaries," or representatives of the bishop of London, to oversee church affairs in America, or on the SPG, which provided ministers and money but lacked authority to govern America's Anglican churches.

These denominational institutions directed the expansion of Quaker, Presbyterian, Baptist, Lutheran, and Reformed congregations and did much to keep colonial Protestantism from exploding into chaos. They approved and sometimes directed the establishment of new congregations, provided preachers, settled disputes within and between congregations, established standards for ministerial conduct, and disciplined wayward ministers and members. For example, when the Baptist congregation at Piscataway, New Jersey, discovered that its minister, Henry Loveall, was a bigamist and an impostor, the Philadelphia Baptist Association helped the congregation select a new minister approved by the Association, noting that Loveall seemed to have chosen an appropriate name for himself.

The denominational institutions also settled—and sometimes heightened—doctrinal and theological disputes. When the Quakers divided over matters of doctrine in the 1690s, the Philadelphia Yearly Meeting settled the affair, and when the Presbyterians debated the merits of revivalism in the 1740s pro-revivalists marched out of the Synod of Philadelphia to form their own Synod of New York.

Authority in the denominations flowed down from the top, not up from the bottom. Ordained ministers conducted the proceedings of all the denominational sessions except the Quaker meetings, because the Quakers did not ordain clergymen. Yet even there, men who were designated to preach publicly dominated the yearly meetings. Lay men and women seldom took part in or even attended denominational meetings. The Presbyterians did not allow a congregation to send a lay representative to these meetings unless the congregation's minister was present, and few congregations sent lay representatives to presbyteries or the Synod of Philadelphia. At the same time, congregations found that they could exercise their own power over clergymen through controlling their ministers' salaries. Because most of these ministers were paid by their listeners rather than by the government, they risked losing their salaries if they displeased their congregations.

On the whole, the denominational institutions in America proved to be far more vigorous than their counterparts in Europe. Through their

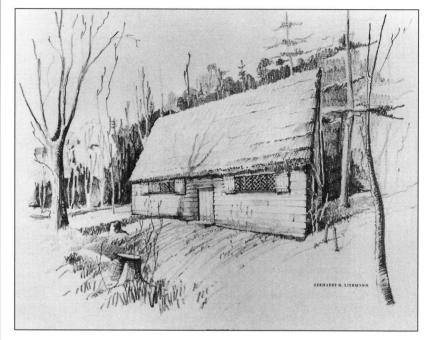

The earliest 17th-century New England meeting houses, like this one in Sudbury, Massachusetts, were very small. They were replaced by much larger and more refined buildings in the 18th century.

emphasis on effective leadership they made an important contribution to the ultimate rise of democracy in America. All of them were modeled on similar institutions in England or Germany—the Quakers' London Yearly Meeting, the London Baptist Association, the numerous presbyteries in England and Scotland, and the organizations of Lutheran and Reformed ministers in the German states. But the number of Baptists and Presbyterians declined in England, and the Quakers' ranks there only held steady, partially drained by the Quaker emigration to Pennsylvania. In Germany, Lutheran and Reformed ministers disagreed about doctrine, revivalism, and the degree to which the churches should have government support.

In America, however, the denominational institutions that were established in the colonies, especially those that grew up in and around Philadelphia, enabled many European religious groups to expand significantly. Colonial Quakers, Presbyterians, Baptists, German Lutherans, and German Reformed denominations increased without colonial governmental support. Between 1680 and 1770 all of them substantially increased the number of congregations affiliated with their groups and raised the membership in their individual congregations.

The expansion of congregational life after 1680 transformed the visual landscape of colonial American religion for all Protestant denominations as well as Catholic and Jewish congregations. The best measure of this transformation is the simplest: Only one or two of the colonial church buildings still seen on the East Coast were constructed before 1680; all the rest were built between 1680 and 1770.

Most churches built before 1680 were small and crude. Few were larger than 20 by 40 or 50 feet, and most featured wood construction, not the stone or brick used in England. For example, the first church constructed in Sudbury, Massachusetts, in 1643, had a thatched roof and measured only 20 by 30 feet. Not until the town's third church was built in 1688 did Sudbury claim a church with a permanent roof and a finished exterior.

Colonial church architecture changed dramatically after 1680 as colonial society expanded dramatically, the economy boomed, and the society became more diverse and sophisticated. Church buildings grew larger and accommodated more people in far more ornate and plush settings. This was true everywhere in the colonies. New England still constructed wooden church buildings, but now they were built on deeper foundations by master craftsmen who raised buildings to staggering heights, often to striking visual effect. The roof in the Old Ship Meeting House in Hingham, Massachusetts, constructed in 1681, spanned a length unimaginable 40 years earlier, and New England churches constructed over the next several decades only grew larger. Churches constructed in the middle and southern colonies after 1680 were equally large, although usually they were brick or stone or had stucco finishes laid over a wood frame.

Regional variations in church architecture also developed after 1680. Maryland and Virginia churches constructed after that year tended to be long and narrow with English and Flemish brickwork that sometimes created zigzag patterns in exterior walls. In contrast, South Carolina's craftsmen more often erected square stucco buildings, like the parish church constructed at St. James Goose Creek in 1706. Before 1740 most rural church buildings could not afford steeples or bells. Congregations that acquired bells usually placed them in wooden stands on the ground and frequently did not build a steeple to house the bells for several decades.

The simple and elegant Anglican parish church in St. James Goose Creek, the oldest surviving Anglican church building in America, was constructed in 1706 for one of South Carolina's wealthiest rural parishes.

The churches constructed after 1680 typically underwent substantial renovation in the next half-century. The Anglican church at St. James Goose Creek may have had a relatively plain interior when it was built in 1706. But by the 1740s it contained a coat of arms of George II, who ascended the British throne in 1727, decorative carved cherubs in gilt paint, a cantilevered pulpit with a mahogany sounding board that amplified the minister's voice, and carefully laid out box pews constructed of fine, polished woods. New England church buildings were no less ornate and featured smoothly polished pews, finely carved pulpits, mahogany baptismal fonts, and silver communion cups.

Synagogues followed similar patterns. New York City's Shearith Israel Synagogue had a women's balcony with high arched windows when it was built in 1730, and Touro Synagogue in Newport, Rhode Island, dedicated in 1763, contained an ornate carved wood interior and finely wrought pews that easily compared with any Christian congregation in the colonies. The Jewish silversmith Myer Myers crafted numerous ceremonial objects, including circumcision instruments and sets of silver Torah ornaments used at Congregation Shearith Israel in New York and Congregation Mikveh Israel in Philadelphia.

Between 1690 and 1770 the colonial cities became centers of ecclesiastical splendor. Although New York City lacked a single church steeple in

Philadelphia's Christ Church, constructed in 1744 by the Church of England, typified the ornate church buildings erected by many Protestant denominations in colonial cities before the American Revolution.

The New York Jewish silversmith Myer Myers made these silver ornaments to ennoble the parchment Torah scroll used in synagogue services at Congregation Mikveh Israel of Philadelphia in the 1770s.

1680, four pierced the skyline by 1720 and more were added in the next decades. In Philadelphia, Anglican, Presbyterian, Baptist, German Lutheran, and German Reformed churches constructed between 1720 and 1750 transformed the skyline of a city previously known only for its quiet Quaker meetinghouses.

By the 1750s Charleston offered the most spectacular example of resplendent church architecture in the American colonies. St. Philip's, the city's first large Anglican church, was constructed in 1720. Then in 1751 an even larger Anglican church, St. Michael's, was built only six blocks to the south of St. Philip's. Both churches had an organ, steeples, bells, hanging lamps, embroidered seat cushions, finely carved pews, and massive columns. If they reflected the wealth gained through slaveholding and trade, they also bespoke the rising power of the European denominations in the 18th-century colonies.

Revivalism among evangelical Protestants challenged and reinforced traditional organized religion in the 18th-century colonies. Distinguished by frequent emotional outpourings and promoting a "born again" religious experience in which participants declared their rebirth as believing Christians, revivals were as controversial in the 18th century as they have been since. Critics found them crude, overly emotional, and anti-intellectual. Supporters viewed revivals as unparalleled opportunities to refresh denominations that were expanding numerically yet lacked inner conviction and fervor.

The colonial revivals had important European origins. They were a far distant expression of the European "pietist" movement that stressed personal religious introspection and individual transformation. This movement originated in Prussia and other German principalities in the 1690s and early 1700s, then extended to the Netherlands and England. It stressed personal religious experience and encouraged individuals to look within to determine their true adherence to Christianity. Aspects of this European revivalism appeared in the 1690s in Northampton, Massachusetts, where the Congregationalist minister Solomon Stoddard sponsored revivals for more than a decade. In the 1720s, similar pietist sentiments supported an intense revivalism in the New Jersey Dutch Reformed congregations led by Theodorus Frelinghuysen. Then, in the 1740s, revivalism seemed to spring up in many places, especially among middle colony Presbyterians and New England Baptists, as well as in the preaching of powerful transatlantic figures like the Anglican revivalist George Whitefield.

Two especially powerful clergymen typified 18th-century colonial revivalism. The Anglican minister George Whitefield became a model for the modern evangelist. This Church of England minister bitterly criticized his own denomination. Other Anglican clergymen treated him as a virtual enemy, yet Whitefield never left the Anglican Church. He was regarded as unusually handsome but had crossed eyes that followers sometimes regarded as a sign of divine promise. And he possessed an actor's voice and an extraordinary sense of public relations that made him the first modern celebrity in America.

Whitefield made seven tours of the British colonies between 1739 and

The Anglican itinerant minister and revivalist George Whitefield preached to thousands of colonists in seven trips to Britain's mainland colonies between 1740 and his death in 1770. Listeners often believed that his crossed eyes marked him as a man of divine gifts.

SINNERS

In the Hands of an

Angry GOD.

A SERMON

Preached at *Enfield*, *July* 8th 1 7 4 1.

At a Time of great Awakenings ; and attended with remarkable Impreſſions on many of the Hearers.

By *Jonathan Edwards*, A.M.

Paſtor of the Church of CHRIST in *Northampton*.

Amos ix. 2, 3. *Though they dig into Hell, thence ſhall mine Hand take them ; though they climb up to Heaven, thence will I bring them down And though they hide themſelves in the Top of Carmel, I will ſearch and take them out thence ; and though they be hid from my Sight in the Bottom of the Sea, thence I will command the Serpent, and he ſhall bite them.*

B O S T O N: Printed and Sold by S. KNEELAND and T. GREEN. in Queen-Street over againſt the Priſon. 1 7 4 1.

Jonathan Edwards's sermon "Sinners in the Hands of an Angry God" (1741) became famous as an example of frightening revival preaching, although Edwards seldom employed its tone and rhetoric again.

his death in Newburyport, Massachusetts, in 1770. He attracted enormous crowds in the colonial cities. Some 10,000 people reputedly flocked to hear him preach in Philadelphia in 1741. Even the skeptical Benjamin Franklin found Whitefield engaging and discovered himself contributing to Whitefield's cause during the evangelist's Philadelphia visit. Whitefield's preaching was distinguished by the simple question he asked over and over: "What must I do to be saved?" This question dominated Whitefield's preaching for 30 years and was central to much of American revivalism for the next two centuries.

Whitefield made major changes in colonial preaching. Before he arrived in America, many colonial preachers wrote their sermons on small pieces of paper that they held close to their eyes when they preached, often reading the sermon in a dull drone for more than an hour. Whitefield gave ministers a new standard. He memorized his sermons and spoke without notes. He varied his voice. He gestured, sometimes calmly, at others in agitation. He held audiences in awe and created the model for modern American revivalists, from Charles Finney in the 19th century to Billy Sunday and Billy Graham in the 20th century.

Jonathan Edwards of western Massachusetts offered another model for the colonial revivalists. Whitefield had little interest in theology, but Edwards became the most important English theologian on either side of the Atlantic in the 18th century. He produced an enormous range of published works that made him internationally known by the time of his death in 1758, the most famous being his books *Freedom of the Will* (1754) and *Original Sin* (1758).

Edwards's importance in the colonial revivals reveals their complexity. In the 1730s Edwards believed that the revivals he was leading and experiencing in Northampton, Massachusetts, reflected the operation of God in human history. He thought the revivals prefaced the second coming of Christ and would usher in a new millennium, or thousand-year reign of Christ on earth. Edwards's most famous revival sermon, "Sinners in the Hands of an Angry God," which he preached in 1741 at the height of the revivals, established the stereotype of the angry, vindictive revival preacher. In it, Edwards so vividly described the destruction of those who were not saved that he had to stop preaching several times because his frightening words convulsed the audience: "Your wickedness makes you as...heavy as lead. [You will] tend downwards with great weight and pressure towards hell, and if God should let you go, you would immediately sink and descend and plunge into the bottomless gulf."

But Edwards also became doubtful about revivals as they progressed. He worried that enthusiastic preachers could too easily lead lay men and women into irresponsible, even blasphemous behavior. For example, James Davenport, a Presbyterian minister who had been trained at Yale, promoted emotional displays of revival activity, encouraged laymen to preach, and burned books and luxury goods in New London, Connecticut, in 1743 as a sign that his followers had adopted a new life. Edwards rejected such radicalism and encouraged ministers to be more careful in their preaching and especially in encouraging emotional outbursts from their listeners.

The revivals, which historians have called the Great Awakening, never were consistent in theology. Early revivalists like the Presbyterian Gilbert Tennent encouraged listeners to reject unconverted ministers. In a well-known sermon he preached in 1740 titled "The Danger of an Unconverted Ministry," Tennent attacked perfunctory, lifeless ministers who knew church doctrine but could not claim a conversion experience. Tennent urged congregations to follow other preachers, including itinerants. But George Whitefield and Jonathan Edwards rejected such views, and Tennent soon changed his own mind. By 1742 Tennent, like Edwards, had come to view itinerant and lay preaching alike with suspicion. He thundered that "ignorant young converts" who preached introduced "the greatest errors and the greatest anarchy and confusion."

Theological diversity also characterized the revivals. Calvinists still believing in predestination dominated the New England revivals. The Dutch Reformed revivals in New Jersey in the 1720s stemmed from pietistic influences from Germany. The Presbyterian revivals in the middle colonies were strongly affected by the charismatic leadership of that denomination's ministers Gilbert, John, and William Tennent. They intimated that they bore special signs of divine favor or even supernatural possession. Gilbert Tennent described how his brother William had once been raised from the dead, and John Tennent was known for his frequent flights of ecstatic, mystical religiosity: "He often took the Bible in his hand, and walked up and down the room, weeping and moaning over it."

Despite the notoriety cast upon them by opponents, the 18th-century colonial religious revivals often were short-lived, tied to local circumstances, and modest in their social and political consequences. Upheavals and schisms, or splits, within churches occurred almost everywhere revivals appeared. In New England the revivals began in the 1730s and ended about 1750. They split the Congregationalists and Baptists into the "New Lights" who backed the revivals and the "Old Lights" who opposed them. English and Scottish Presbyterians carried on most of the revivals in the middle colonies, but the Baptists were almost completely unaffected by revivals in those colonies. These revivals split the middle colony Presbyterians just as they had New England's Congregationalists and Baptists. Proponents of revivals walked out of the Synod of Philadelphia and formed a rival Synod of New York in 1745. The revivalists demanded higher standards for ministers in personal life and guarantees that their ministers were indeed "born again." Only moral and regenerate ministers could preach with conviction, they argued. The breach between the two synods was not healed until 1758.

Revivals in the southern colonies produced confrontations between the Church of England and evangelical Baptists and Methodists. Unlike revivals in most other colonies, those in Virginia and Maryland exploited

Jonathan Edwards
Rouses a Congregation

Jonathan Edwards preached this sermon, "Sinners in the Hands of an Angry God," during a revival in Enfield, Massachusetts, in 1741. He sought to impress his listeners with a simple, terrifying idea: that only God and nothing else kept them from eternal damnation. The sermon was far more negative and frightening than any of Edwards's other sermons, but it has long been his most famous writing.

Jonathan Edwards had become famous throughout British religious circles by 1750, and this portrait was commissioned by admirers in Edinburgh, Scotland.

Natural men are held in the hand of God over the pit of hell; they have deserved the fiery pit, and are already sentenced to it; and God is dreadfully provoked, his anger is as great towards them as to those that are actually suffering the executions of the fierceness of his wrath in hell....

You probably are not sensible of this; you find you are kept out of hell, but don't see the hand of God in it, but look at other things, as the good state of your bodily constitution, your care of your own life, and the means you use for your own preservation. But indeed these things are nothing; if God should withdraw his hand, they would avail no more to keep you from falling, than the thin air to hold up a person that is suspended in it.

Your wickedness makes you as it were heavy as lead, and to tend downwards with great weight and pressure towards hell; and if God should let you go, you would immediately sink and swiftly descend and plunge into the bottomless gulf, and your healthy constitution, and your own care and prudence, and best contrivance, and all your righteousness, would have no more influence to uphold you and keep you out of hell, than a spider's web would have to stop a falling rock.

Around 1775, when she was 16, Prudence Punderson made this needlepoint depicting a young colonial woman's view of life from birth (on the right) to death (on the left). In fact, Punderson died only a decade later, at age 26.

social and political tensions in the colony. Baptists, and later Methodists, openly appealed to poorer, often illiterate farmers and to enslaved Africans. They directly attacked the Church of England, whose large, ornate churches by then symbolized the powerful status they had achieved in both colonies. In contrast, the Baptists and Methodists often preached outdoors or in private homes. Their crude, plain churches only heightened their differences with the Anglicans.

Women's roles changed in colonial religion as the denominations expanded and as revivalism rose and fell. These changes were subtle rather than dramatic. But they held important implications for American religion well into the 19th century. These changes quietly altered the overwhelming power of men in colonial religion. In both the 17th and 18th centuries women could not be ordained as ministers in any colonial religious group, and in all groups except the Quakers women could conduct no formal meetings or hold regular offices in colonial congregations and denominations. This meant that it was extremely difficult for women to influence colonial congregational life directly in ways available to men. Such conditions were not unexpected, because they paralleled women's status in secular life. In the 18th century women could not vote. Women lost their property rights when they married, and women often had to have men manage property for them even when they had inherited it or purchased it themselves.

One fact made women's situation in colonial religion unusual, however: after 1680 women made up between 55 and 70 percent of the membership in most Congregational, Baptist, and German Lutheran congregations and probably constituted the majority of listeners in the remaining congregations. This was true from New England to South Carolina and from east to west. Just why women outnumbered men in the colonial congregations is not clear. One observation explains at least part of the pattern, however: Women joined congregations at much younger ages than men, often in their early twenties, while men frequently delayed joining until their thirties and forties. As a result, women sometimes outnumbered men two to one in many colonial congregations.

Colonial Quakers and Baptists, however, gave women more direct roles in their denominations and presaged the rise of women's religious activity in 19th- and 20th-century America. The Quakers in England and America created special women's meetings within their overall form of denominational government. They were the only English denomination to do so. It was the Quakers' theology that made this possible. George Fox, the founder of the Quaker movement, wrote that after the fall of Adam, "man was to rule over his wife." But "in the restoration by Christ," which the Quakers believed they were accomplishing, "they are help-meets, man and woman, as they were before the fall."

In this role as "help-meets," Quaker women regularly handled two important issues in their women's meetings: charity and marriage. The women's meetings made arrangements to take care of the elderly poor of both sexes, cared for widows, found homes for orphaned children, and gave cash to the destitute. They disciplined not only women members but men as well when they violated Quaker marriage regulations. In fact, most Quaker discipline cases focused on marriage to non-Quakers, or marrying "out of unity with Friends," as the Quakers put it. When these marriages reached epidemic proportions in Pennsylvania in the early 1750s, the women's and men's meetings cooperated to disown wayward Quakers. The women's meetings initiated the disownments, and the men's meetings reviewed and regularly upheld them. The Quaker women's meetings were not independent of the men's meetings, but the men's meetings recognized and honored the authority of the women's meetings. By the early 19th century, the women's meetings and the women who conducted them had become the foundations of an extraordinary activism among Quaker women that helped create the American tradition of social activism and humanitarianism.

The Baptists sometimes allowed women to vote in congregational matters, especially in New England and sometimes in Pennsylvania. "New Light" Baptist congregations formed in New England during the revivals of the 1730s and 1740s often allowed women members to vote on congregational affairs. In doing so, women spoke publicly about a variety of issues important to congregational life, including the disciplining of sinful members for sexual misconduct, "pridefulness," theft, and unorthodox preaching. Women also voted to help select ministers and participated in the process of the "washing of feet," a ritual adopted in some Baptist congregations to symbolize the equality of all believers.

When challenged, women defended their right to vote. Once, when men in the Philadelphia Baptist Congregation tried to prevent women from voting in congregational matters in 1764, the women responded vigorously. One of them, Joanna Anthony, wrote that if the women had "thought their privilege or their practices contrary to the word of God they would or ought to have kept themselves separate from them." For the moment, at least, Philadelphia's Baptist women retained their voting rights.

This Baptist experiment in congregational government did not last, however. After the American Revolution, Baptist congregations stopped allowing women to vote, perhaps because the Baptists became more con-

ventional as they moved farther away from their 18th-century revivalist enthusiasm. Yet like the example of the Quakers, the mid-18th-century Baptist example looked forward to greater women's activism and assertiveness in 19th-century American religion. Belief in the outright religious equality of men and women, symbolized in a willingness to ordain women to the ministry, did not occur until the late 20th century in most American religious groups.

Women also played interesting, and sometimes vital, roles in other colonial churches where they could not vote or lacked special meetings. Their centrality in home life gave them important roles in funerals, baptisms, and weddings, many of which were performed in the home and were often managed by women, although men conducted the services. Women frequently managed the religious education of children, especially because there were no special services for children and the Sunday

In 18th-century Quaker meetings a woman's voice carried the same weight as a man's, distinguishing the Society of Friends from other religious groups of the period.

Sarah Osborn Leads African-American Religious Revivals

In the colonial period, very few women were allowed to exercise religious leadership in Christian congregations, although they usually made up 60 to 70 percent of the congregational membership. Sarah Osborn challenged this pattern in Newport, Rhode Island, in the mid 1760s. A white schoolteacher who supported her family when her merchant husband went bankrupt, Mrs. Osborn began leading religious "exercises" in 1766–67 among the town's numerous African slaves. Initially, she faced vigorous criticism for her work and acted cautiously to win support, as she reported in this letter to a supporter, Rev. Joseph Fish of Stonington, Connecticut. Within several months, Osborn was also leading religious meetings among Newport whites with as many as 500 people in attendance.

I will begin with the great [work] respecting the poor Blacks on Lord's day evenings, which above all the rest has been exercising to my mind. And first let me assure you sir, it would be the joy of my heart to commit it into superior hands did any arise for their help. My reverend pastor and brethren are my witnesses that I have earnestly sought, yea in bitterness of soul, for their assistance and protection. [I] would gladly be under inspection of pastor and church and turn things into a safe channel. O forever blessed be my gracious God that has Himself vouchsafed to be my protection hitherto by putting his fear into my heart and thereby moving me as far as possible in this surprising day.…I only read to them, talk to them, and sing a psalm or hymn with them, and then at eight o'clock dismiss them all by name as upon list. They call it school, and I had rather it should be called almost any thing that is good than [the word] meeting, I [am so reluctant to be the] head of any thing that bears that name.... The poor creatures attend with so much decency and quietness you might almost hear as we say the shaking of a leaf when there is more than an hundred under the roof at once.

I know of no one in the town now that is against me.... Every intimate brother and friend intreats and charges me not to dismiss [the meetings] so long as things rest as they are, telling me it would be the worst days work that ever I did if I should, as God Himself has thus employed me. If any disturbance or disorder should arise either to the breaking of public or family peace, that would immediately make the path of duty plain for dismissing at once, but on the contrary ministers and magistrates send their servants and approve.

S. Osborn

February 28, 1767

Protestant women's charitable work in early 19th-century America stimulated societies to promote education and temperance and support orphans, which Harriet Sewell's watercolor "The Orphans" commemorated in 1808.

school would not be created until the 1820s. Finally, women were frequently extremely well informed on religious issues, and men and women often discussed religious issues in each other's company. Not all these conversations went well. Ann Carter sometimes so irritated her husband, a wealthy Virginia planter named William Byrd, with her contrary religious views that Byrd skipped his own nightly prayers when they argued.

Yet the predominance of women in most colonial congregations and the late age at which men joined congregations gave rise to two situations. Rightly or wrongly, men often thought of women as more "naturally" religious. And women persistently informed themselves on religion and theology despite their exclusion in most denominations from the pulpit and formal church business.

In all, the decades between 1680 and 1770 changed American religion in fundamental ways. The number of individual congregations greatly multiplied, and the various denominational institutions expanded. Revivals that were markedly different in theology and style tore some religious groups apart and thrust others into bitter interdenominational contests. While women lacked authority and power in most denominations, they continued to constitute a majority of church members in virtually all denominations. Within two denominations, the Quakers and Baptists, 18th-century women created important models for increased religious activity in the 19th century when women managed philanthropic and reform groups and demanded the right to preach. In these ways, the 18th century witnessed the birth of important distinctive traits—denominational aggressiveness, revivalism, and women's religious activism—that typified American religion in the next three centuries.

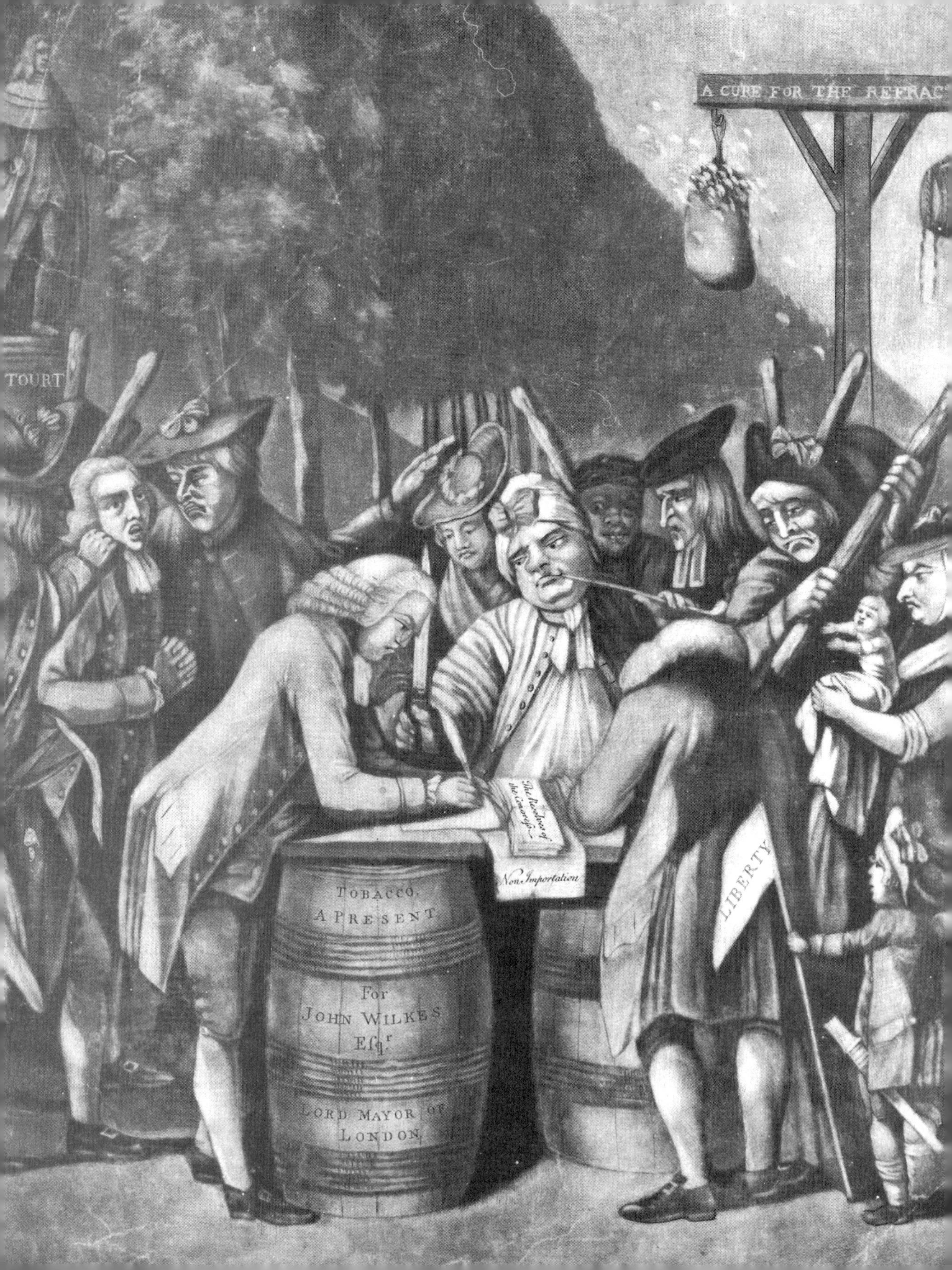

A CURE FOR THE REFRAC
TOURT
The Resolves of the Assembly
Non Importation
TOBACCO
A PRESENT
For
JOHN WILKES
Esq.r
LORD MAYOR OF
LONDON
LIBERTY

Chapter 6

Religion and the American Revolution

At its heart, the American Revolution was a profoundly secular event. The Declaration of Independence said little about religion. Instead, it discussed disputes over English parliamentary authority, the rights of colonial legislatures, and foolish mistakes made by English politicians.

Yet religion played interesting, occasionally surprising, and sometimes contradictory roles in the American Revolution. Moreover, the Revolution deeply affected religion in America far beyond 1776. By 1791 the first U.S. Congress passed the Bill of Rights, or the first ten amendments to the new federal Constitution, including the First Amendment, which prohibited any governmental establishment of religion and guaranteed freedom of worship in the new republic.

The First Amendment looked in two directions simultaneously. It confirmed the diverse and vigorous religious expressions created in the colonial period and guaranteed that government would not engage in religious activity itself. For the future, it freed religion from government, and government from religion, in unprecedented ways never proposed by any society, Old World or New.

Both paths were novel. Some people believed they were dangerous. But few doubted that they embodied the essence of colonial American religious development—the evolution of a lively, multifaceted, multiracial, multiethnic religious world brought forth mainly by independent groups and individuals rather than by the state.

Religion affected the American Revolution, but religion did not cause the Revolution. The Declaration of Independence, signed on July 4, 1776, best expresses the secular character of the Revolution. Religion entered into the Declaration only in the phrase "the laws of nature and nature's God," and in references to "Divine Providence" (on which Americans would rely for protection) and to "the Supreme Judge of the world" (who would judge the "rectitude of our intentions"). Nowhere did Thomas Jefferson, its principal author, refer simply to "God" alone or to Christ. He did not invoke Christian doctrine in support of the Revolution. Not a single religious issue found a place in the long "history of repeated injuries and usurpations" at the end of the Declaration where Jefferson described the misbehavior of the British.

This seeming omission is surprising, because at least one religious issue played an interesting role in fostering anti-English feeling in the colonies. This was the so-called bishop question. This term referred to a proposal made several times in the 1710s, the 1750s, and then again in the 1760s to name a bishop to preside over the Church of England in the colonies. The Boston Congregationalist minister Jonathan Mayhew preached against the appointment of an Anglican bishop in 1750. He stressed the danger of "imperious bishops" and used the word "tyranny" four or five times on a single page to describe Anglican intentions.

The controversy escalated in 1761 when a new Anglican minister in Cambridge, Massachusetts, built a large mansion for himself that was seemingly beyond the reach of a mere parish clergyman. Congregationalist opponents of the Church of England dubbed it the "bishop's palace." They claimed that the Anglicans were on the verge of naming a bishop who would destroy religious liberty, convene ecclesiastical courts to try colonists for religious offenses, and use government funds to promote Anglican causes. Actually, Anglicans sought the appointment of a "suffragan" bishop who, by law, could administer Anglican church matters but had no authority to convene ecclesiastical courts or exercise governmental power.

No Anglican bishop was ever appointed, but the "bishop question" became a part of anti-English agitation for the next decade. In 1763 and 1764 the possible appointment of an Anglican bishop joined colonial protests against stamps and taxes. In 1774 colonists linked the bishop question to protests against the Quebec Act in which the English government recognized the Catholic Church in the conquered French territories of Canada, where most settlers were Catholic. But in the old British mainland colonies, the Quebec Act conjured up fears that Catholics and a tyrannical Church of England would steal America's religious freedom.

The Boston silversmith and engraver Paul Revere graphically exploited these fears in a 1774 cartoon. In it, the Devil hovers over Anglican bishops and members of Parliament plotting to achieve their long-secret objective of catholicizing the American colonies. In fact, the bishop question became a major issue only in New England and New York. In other colonies, where the Anglican presence was larger, especially those from Maryland down to South Carolina, the bishop question held little interest. Delegates to the Continental Congress did not mention it in the Declaration of Independence adopted in July 1776.

Before the Revolution, religion reinforced popular arguments about the need for virtue and morality in society and politics. In politics, this was called Whiggism, because it overlapped the rhetoric of England's 18th-century Whig political party. Several important political tracts widely distributed in the colonies supported this view, especially *Cato's*

This cartoon of a half-soldier, half-bishop landing in Boston in the 1770s protested British enforcement of navigation and tax laws and alleged Anglican attempts to take away colonists' religious freedom.

When John Singleton Copley painted this portrait of the silversmith Paul Revere admiring one of his superb silver chocolate pots in 1770, he had little idea of the patriotic fame Revere would achieve during the American Revolution.

Letters, written in the 1720s by two English authors, John Trenchard and Thomas Gordon.

A wide variety of colonial clergymen reinforced Whig political ideals. Throughout the 18th century, the public discussion of virtue and morality came most often from clergymen. Laymen and clergymen alike assumed that political liberty depended on having a virtuous public. The ministers emphasized virtue, responsibility, and the importance of moral choices. In doing so, they created important standards that colonists used to criticize English actions in the 1760s and 1770s.

For example, when the Maryland Anglican clergyman John Gordon preached against tyranny and in favor of virtue and morality in government in the mid-1740s, his text bristled with allusions to Whig political literature. Gordon and other clergymen from Massachusetts to South Carolina stressed the work necessary to sustain private morality and virtue in public life and politics. As Thomas Cradock, another Maryland Anglican minister, put it, "Virtue is a rich prey rescued narrowly out of the fire." Virtue had to be maintained by the "purchase of labor and sweat of care and vigilance. We are too liable to lose it by our own sloth and treachery."

These standards came into play even before the British began to tinker with the empire after 1763. Many colonists were repelled by the behavior of British "regulars" sent from England to fight in the so-called French and Indian War of 1758-63. Colonial ministers were not silent on the topic. John Cleveland of Ipswich, Massachusetts, who served as a chaplain, or minister, to soldiers during the war, complained that "profane swearing seems to be the naturalized language of the regulars." Their "gaming, robbery, [and] thievery" epitomized the immorality and corruption that colonists feared was rampant in English society.

Between 1763 and 1776, especially in New England, some ministers discussed colonial politics and protests in their sermons as the level of colonial political protest escalated. A few ministers who supported the colonial cause argued that the colonists' own immorality brought them God's wrath in the form of English tyranny. One New England minister proclaimed that "it is for a people's sins when God suffers this evil to come upon them."

Other ministers supported the colonists more enthusiastically. The Massachusetts Loyalist Peter Oliver laid the blame for New England's anti-British sentiment on "black coated mobs," clergymen who preached anti-English sermons from their tax-supported pulpits. One observer claimed that Philadelphia's ministers "thunder and lighten every sabbath" with anti-English sermons. The wealthy Virginia planter Landon Carter reported that his own Anglican parish minister, who might have been expected to support the Crown, exhorted listeners "to support their Liberties ... and in the room of 'God save the king,' he cried out 'God preserve all the just rights and liberties of America.'"

But most colonial ministers remained silent about politics during the upheavals of the 1760s and 1770s. The Presbyterians exhibited a particularly mixed record on the Revolution. John Witherspoon, a Presbyterian

Paul's Revere's commitment to the colonists' cause led him to engrave this satirical cartoon lampooning the Crown's support for Catholicism in French Canada in the Quebec Act of 1774. The Devil is overlooking the proceedings.

Loyalists sometimes attached religious meaning to their cause. This drawing depicted their arrival in Britain in 1783, with angels approving their suffering in America for the cause of both Crown and Church.

minister who was president of the College of New Jersey (later renamed Princeton), wrote against the English and attended the Continental Congress as a delegate. Several other Presbyterian ministers also supported the colonists in the 1760s and 1770s and described the Revolutionary War as a battle between Christ and Antichrist, with Christ supporting the colonists, of course.

Yet most Presbyterian clergymen remained aloof from revolutionary fervor as late as 1775. The Synod of Philadelphia reflected their ambivalence about the war. The 1775 synod acknowledged that it was "well known…that we have not been instrumental in inflaming the minds of the people." Many of the ministers were Scots. They worried that any possible war would be like the bloody civil war that had ravaged Scotland in the 1740s, which they warned was "carried on with a rancor and spirit of revenge much greater than [wars] between independent states." Presbyterians expressed their "attachment and respect to our sovereign King George" and to the "person of the prince." They believed he may have been misled in his actions toward the colonies. But they also rejected "such insults as have been offered to the sovereign" by many colonial protesters.

German Lutheran and Reformed clergymen in Pennsylvania also exhibited misgivings about the Revolution. They were a minority in the colony, and their occasional disputes with Pennsylvania's leading politicians, who now led anti-English protests, dampened their enthusiasm for independence. They also worried about the possible effects of the upheavals on both Christianity and America. In May 1775 the German Reformed Coetus, the organization of Reformed ministers, warned lay men and women about the "precarious times" in which they lived, "the like of which…has never been seen in America." In 1777 the Coetus still described the Revolution as a "sad war" that had uprooted "the keeping of the Sabbath day and Christian exercises in the families at home."

Open loyalism to the king was evident most obviously in the Church of England. Anglicans, both ministers and lay men and women, supported the Crown for the simplest of reasons: The king was the head of the church, and the church, like all other churches, had long taught obedience to constituted authority. Similar loyalism also cropped up among some New England Congregationalists and occasional Presbyterians and Baptists, although these expressions proved rare.

A second kind of loyalism stemmed from long-standing antagonism between dominant religious groups and minorities, especially in backcountry settlements. Scots and Scots-Irish Presbyterians in the western Carolinas, English Baptists in Virginia, German Lutherans and German Reformed groups in Pennsylvania, and Anglicans in New England all had experienced antagonism from the dominant religious groups in their regions. They often found the patriots' antiparliamentary protests hypocritical. Some groups, especially Virginia's Baptists, who had struggled for

Presbyterian Caution about the American Revolution

During the political crisis with England between 1763 and 1776, some American minis-
ters consistently supported the colonists' cause. Most, however, said nothing, and the
Revolution split groups like the Quakers, some of whom abandoned their traditional
pacifism to fight for independence.

In May 1775 Presbyterians who had gathered in their yearly synod or administra-
tive council in Philadelphia devoted much of their annual "pastoral letter" to the dispute
with England. The ministers concluded with a commitment to settling the dispute on
"constitutional principles." But their experience in the 1740s with violent civil war in
Scotland between Scots loyal to Britain and others supporting James II, the Catholic pre-
tender to the Scottish throne, led the ministers to warn their congregations about the
dangers and violence of the coming contest.

Very Dear Brethren:

The Synod of New York and Philadelphia...have long seen with concern, the circumstances which occasioned, and the gradual increase of this unhappy difference.
As ministers of the gospel of peace, we have ardently wished that it could, and
often hoped that it would have been more early accommodated. It is well known to
you...that we have not been instrumental in inflaming the minds of the people, or
urging them to acts of violence and disorder. Perhaps no instance can be given on

so interesting a subject, in which political sentiments have been so long and so fully kept from the pulpit....

We think it of importance, at this time, to recommend to all of every rank, but especially to those who may be called to action, a spirit of humanity and mercy. Every battle of the warrior is with confused noise, and garments rolled in blood. It is impossible to appeal to the sword without being exposed to many scenes of cruelty and slaughter; but it is often observed, that civil wars are carried on with a rancour and spirit of revenge much greater than those between independent States. The injuries received, or supposed, in civil wars, wound more deeply than those of foreign enemies[;] it is therefore the more necessary to guard against this abuse, and recommend that meekness and gentleness of spirit, which is the noblest attendant on true valour. That man will fight most bravely, who never fights till it is necessary, and who ceases to fight as soon as the necessity is over....

We conclude with our most earnest prayer, that the God of heaven may bless you in your temporal and spiritual concerns, and that the present unnatural dispute may be speedily terminated by an equitable and lasting settlement on constitutional principles.

Signed in the name, presence, and by appointment of the Synod.
Benjamin Hait, Moderator.
New York, May 22d, 1775

a decade with the colony's Anglican church, supported the Revolution nonetheless. But many of the others either remained neutral or openly supported the Crown.

Of course, most colonists supported independence. In doing so, religion followed politics rather than leading it. Yet religion offered important rhetoric in support of the Revolutionary cause. A New York Presbyterian, Abraham Keteltas, called the Revolution "the cause of heaven against hell." A South Carolina Baptist, Elhanan Winchester, described English actions as motivated by "Rome and Hell."

Some clergymen added a new dimension to Revolutionary rhetoric in the form of millennialism. Millennialist beliefs asserted Christ's imminent return to earth to carry out a thousand-year reign, and they had surfaced occasionally in the colonial period, especially in the revivals of the 1740s. But the political turmoil between 1763 and 1776 recharged these beliefs. According to this way of thinking, the Revolution was a matter of religious, not just secular, significance. One Connecticut clergyman, Ebenezer Baldwin, believed that Christ's return to earth was imminent and that the Revolution was "preparing the way for this glorious event." A New Hampshire minister thought the Revolution fulfilled certain second-coming predictions in the Old Testament book of Isaiah.

Most clergymen and lay men and women looked upon such beliefs with skepticism. Yet the rise of millennialist thinking during the Revolution had two important consequences. For one, it initiated a pattern common in American wars, from the Civil War to the Vietnam War, that associated God with America's cause. Secondly, it sometimes interpreted these wars as signs of Christ's return to earth. To some people these views demonstrated the Revolution's links to religion, even though only a tiny minority of Revolutionary-era Americans ever embraced millennialism.

The Revolutionary War proved difficult for some denominations. Predictably, the Church of England suffered the most. The colonial protests and the Revolutionary War destroyed the patient work that had enlarged the Anglican following in the previous century. About 75 percent of the Church of England congregations lost their clergymen. Anglican ministers in parish after parish left because they supported the

Crown and could not endure continued abuse by local patriots. And the physical destruction loosed on Anglican churches was similar to that against Catholic churches in 17th-century Maryland. Revolutionaries ripped out royal coats of arms from the walls of many Anglican churches and murdered an Anglican minister in Rye, New York.

Baptists also experienced substantial problems during the Revolution. The war disrupted local congregational life and activity. In 1776 the Philadelphia Baptist Association counted 42 congregations with 3,000 members. But in 1781 the association's rolls had declined to 26 congregations with only 1,400 members. Many congregations disbanded, and the surviving ones lost significant membership, with the average congregation declining from 71 to 55 members.

The Quakers split over the Revolution, especially in Pennsylvania. One group called the Free Quakers backed independence and rejected the traditional Quaker pacifism. Quaker leaders viewed the call to arms and the violence of the Revolution as abhorrent to Quaker principles. Friends found themselves hunted down in the very colony they had founded. In May 1776 a stone-throwing mob forced Philadelphia Quakers to observe a fast day declared by the Continental Congress. A patriot mob in Berks County shackled and jailed a Quaker preacher until he posted a $10,000 bond that guaranteed his "good" behavior, meaning that he would stop encouraging Quakers not to fight. Philadelphia leaders exiled 17 Quakers to Virginia for two years so they would not interfere with revolutionary activities.

Presbyterians suffered at the hands of the British, who burned three Presbyterian churches in New York, two in Connecticut, and five in New Jersey, including the church led by pro-Revolutionary Presbyterian clergyman John Witherspoon. At Huntington, New York, English troops headquartered themselves in the local Presbyterian church and used tombstones as the floor for an oven that left funereal inscriptions on the bread they baked.

Even ministers who supported the Revolution bemoaned the immorality it seemed to foster. During the war years, the Synod of Philadelphia spoke of "gross immoralities," an "increasing decay of vital

In the 1775 anti-American cartoon "A Society of Patriotic Ladies," Philip Dawes lampooned women's political activity, possibly in Edenton, North Carolina, in a boycott of tea.

piety," a "degeneracy of manners," and a "want of public spirit." Baptists in Virginia, South Carolina, and New England decried what they saw as spreading sin and immorality amid the Revolution.

Revolutionary War chaplains frequently experienced highly mixed reactions to their work. Some chaplains found soldiers receptive to their preaching. Religious soldiers appreciated the chaplains' sermons in part because they were reminders of the spiritual rituals they knew at home.

But other chaplains encountered apathy and even open rejection from their soldiers. "It don't seem like Sabbath day,...none seem to know or think any thing about it," wrote one chaplain near Albany, New York. A Rhode Island chaplain "made out miserably" when he preached to battle-weary wounded soldiers. A New England chaplain responded with resignation about his task: "Encourage [the soldiers] when doing their duty, attend and pray...with them when sick, and bury them when they die."

The difficulties many religious groups experienced during the Revolutionary War did not prepare Americans for the marked resurgence in religious activity that occurred after the war ended in 1783. All the denominations, including even the old Church of England, renewed themselves with remarkable vigor. America's religious groups saw their mission as even more important in the new republic than it had been in the old British empire. The freedom promised by independence required even more moral and spiritual guidance. The new republic depended by definition on "a virtuous people," a phrase that circulated throughout all forms of political discussion in the 1780s. Who better to create that "virtuous people" than America's religious denominations?

American religious groups acted quickly to support the new society and government as the patriots' success mounted despite earlier doubts about political revolution and the effects of war. Between 1783 and 1800 clergymen preached hundreds of sermons commemorating the war, praising America's soldiers, and directing its government toward moral and spiritual ends. Fasting and thanksgiving day sermons continued and even increased. Everywhere, ministers proclaimed the fusion that came out of American independence and organized religion, especially Christianity.

Denominational growth resumed after independence. The Presbyterian Synod of Philadelphia expanded from 153 to 215 churches between 1774 and 1788. The Baptists in South Carolina doubled their congregations between 1775 and 1790 and even experienced some congregational expansion during the Revolutionary War itself. In 1785 the Church of England became the Protestant Episcopal Church headed by a bishop elected by American ministers, who was loyal to America, not to England or the British king. Although internal squabbles and lingering resentment over Anglican opposition to independence slowed the Episcopalian recovery, under new leaders the church experienced substantial expansion after about 1810.

Catholicism and Judaism also expanded after the war. John Carroll of Maryland became "superior of the missions" in the former colonies in 1784, replacing London's Vicar Apostolate as the coordinator of Catholic efforts in America. In 1790 Carroll became the first Roman Catholic bishop in the United States, supervising some 65 congregations.

Jewish congregations also grew in number, but not always in size. The congregation in Newport, Rhode Island, declined as the city's economic fortunes withered. However, Jews in Savannah, Georgia, organized a congregation there in 1791, Jews in Philadelphia and Charleston built synagogues in those cities in 1782 and 1794, and New York's Jews reorganized their congregation in 1790 and rebuilt their synagogue in 1817.

The Methodists sustained unusually dramatic growth after the Revolutionary War. In the 1770s the Methodist movement was seriously hobbled by the loyalist Toryism of John Wesley, its leader. Wesley, who firmly supported the king in the revolutionary struggle, recalled the Methodist preachers in the colonies to England, and all but one complied. Francis Asbury, however, continued preaching in the colonies and supported independence. After the war, Methodism boomed. New ministers arrived from England, others were recruited in America, and the Methodist "circuit" system managed by Asbury and others attracted thousands of new followers through highly coordinated preaching tours. In 1784 the Methodists had scarcely 15,000 followers. By 1790, the movement counted almost 60,000 members. By 1810 the Methodists had nearly 150,000 members.

Baptists became the largest single religious group in America after the Revolution. The Baptists never used the strong central organization that the Methodists perfected. Baptist congregations remained relatively independent, joined in loosely affiliated associations modeled on the Philadelphia Baptist Association formed in 1707. But like the Methodists, the Baptists also preached to poor whites and enslaved and free Africans. The fervency of the Baptists' modestly educated preachers, not their formal learning, drew extraordinary crowds. In turn, the Baptist associations

quickly drew new congregations into their midst, secured pastors, and created a sense of belonging without imposing an overbearing, centralized church government. Baptist membership skyrocketed. The denomination numbered 35,000 members in 1784, 65,000 in 1790, and more than 170,000 in 1810.

The growth in church membership in the several decades after the Revolution signaled a slow rise in church membership in America that reached its peak in the 20th century. As the Revolutionary era ended, probably no more than 20 percent of America's adults were church members, although occasional church attendance pushed contact with Christian congregations a little higher. Among whites, South Carolina had the highest rate of church membership; about a third of its white adults belonged to Christian congregations. The percentage of adult whites who were church members ranged from 10 percent in Vermont, the lowest, to

Methodist camp meetings drew thousands of listeners in the early republic and accounted for the Methodist movement's dramatic growth as the new nation emerged.

about 20 percent, the average. The vast majority of enslaved and free African Americans belonged to no Christian congregation, but neither did most whites. This situation changed over the next two centuries. Denominational evangelizing initiated after the Revolution brought church membership in the United States to between 30 and 40 percent by the 1840s. This figure finally topped 50 percent sometime in the early 20th century, then slowly climbed to about 65 percent in the 1950s, where it largely remained to the end of the 20th century.

The involvement of government in religion declined as the denominations expanded. The experience of colonial religious diversity, the failures of the old religious establishments, the association of the Church of England with the king and Parliament, and the principles of the Declaration of Independence all encouraged Americans to rethink the relationship between government and religion as the Revolution proceeded. The old Anglican Church lost most in this reevaluation. Between 1776 and 1785 the legal establishments it had won 80 years earlier in colonies from New York to Maryland, Virginia, and North and South Carolina all collapsed.

Originally, the First Amendment, which banned any state-supported religion, applied only to the federal government. As a result, many states experienced important struggles over government establishment of religion in their own locales. New England dissenters had earlier attacked the establishment of the Congregational Church in Massachusetts and Connecticut, but their battle against governmental involvement in religion generally took much longer. In part, this happened because the newly formed state legislatures removed some of the immediate discontent by exempting Presbyterians, Baptists, Quakers, and Episcopalians from parish church taxes. But the new constitution approved by Connecticut voters in 1818 eliminated the old church establishment. Massachusetts finally abolished its weakened religious establishment in 1833. As in Connecticut, it had become ineffective and stimulated endless lawsuits when established churches splintered and their members bickered over who would retain the church's tax revenues.

The most momentous contest over the establishment of religion occurred in Virginia between 1779 and 1785. This debate centered on two issues: "multiple establishment," or government support for several Protestant groups, and complete disestablishment. In 1779 and again in 1784, Virginia's proponents of multiple establishment, including some Presbyterians and the fiery Revolutionary leader Patrick Henry, introduced bills to provide government support and tax funds for several, but not all, Protestant groups. Henry and the supporters of multiple establishment also proposed limited freedom of worship for all those who recognized one God, believed in future punishment and reward, and supported public worship.

In contrast, Thomas Jefferson offered a bill in 1779 "for Establishing Religious Freedom." It prohibited tax levies for "any religious worship, place, or ministry whatsoever" and also upheld freedom of worship for all religious groups. As the act put it, "All men shall be free to profess, and by argument to maintain, their opinions in matters of religion." Both sides struggled over these issues from 1779 to 1785 without resolution.

A great public debate in 1784–85 effectively stopped the call for multiple establishment, prohibited direct government funding for religious activity, and promoted full religious freedom. James Madison vigorously attacked any government aid for religion in his famous petition "Memorial and Remonstrance against Religious Assessments," which he sent to Virginia's House of Burgesses in 1785. In it he called religion an "unalienable right" of each individual that no government could usurp. Petitions containing more than 10,000 signatures opposed multiple establishment and government aid to select Protestant groups. Baptists especially opposed government aid to religion. Rockbridge County, Virginia, petitioners argued that "religion and all of its duties…ought not to be made the object of human legislation." A Cumberland County petition argued that the early Christians had prospered "for several hundred years without the aid of a civil power" but that corruption had followed after Christianity

Patrick Henry introduced bills in 1779 to give tax support to several Protestant groups in Virginia, but the House of Burgesses rejected the proposals as reminiscent of the old Anglican establishment.

became the official religion of the Roman Empire. What did this history teach? The Cumberland County petitioners had a simple answer: "Religious establishment has never been a means of prospering the Gospel."

The debate completely altered public opinion in Virginia. George Washington's turnaround symbolized the transformation. At first, Washington supported multiple establishment. He initially thought it was a fine idea to give government aid to some Protestant groups. But as the debate proceeded he changed his mind and turned against the proposal. Multiple establishment, Washington commented, seemed so innocuous and natural but would "rankle, and perhaps convulse the state." As a result, in 1786 the Virginia legislature rejected Patrick Henry's bill for multiple establishment. Overwhelming opposition to it came from Baptists, Methodists, Episcopalians, and some Presbyterians. The legislature then approved by a vote of 74 to 20 Thomas Jefferson's bill "for Establishing Religious Freedom." It outlawed government aid to religion and guaranteed freedom of worship to all religions in the state, not just Protestants or even Christians.

The Virginia debate speeded the decline of the multiple-establishment proposals that had at first seemed attractive in other states. South Carolina's 1778 constitution had authorized government aid to several Protestant groups. But its 1790 constitution abandoned multiple establishment and guaranteed "the free exercise and enjoyment of religious profession and worship, without discrimination or preference." Within a year, the state had chartered Charleston's Jewish congregation, Beth Elochim. Multiple-establishment bills failed in Georgia in 1782 and 1784. Government aid to several Protestant groups was approved in 1785 but was never implemented, and in 1789 a new Georgia constitution eliminated multiple religious establishment. The post-Revolutionary Maryland constitution permitted multiple establishment, but the state's legislature never approved such aid. It rejected funding for Protestant groups by a 2-to-1 margin in 1785 and in 1810 eliminated multiple establishment through an amendment to the state constitution.

In New Hampshire, government aid to local Protestant congregations slowly collapsed because of the local disputes it caused. By 1815 half the

S I R,

The following Act, which was paſſed in the ASSEMBLY OF VIRGINNIA, at the beginning of this year, affords an example of legiſlative wiſdom and liberality never before known, and muſt pleaſe all the friends of intellectual and religious liberty. It was lately printed at PARIS; and you will do an important ſervice by aſſiſting in circulating it. Had the principles which have dictated it, been always acted upon by civil governments, the demon of perſecution would never have exiſted; ſincere enquiries would never have been diſcouraged; truth and reaſon would have had fair play; and moſt of the evils which have diſturbed the peace of the world, and obſtructed human improvement, would have been prevented.

NEWINGTON-GREEN, July 26, 1786.   R. P.

An Act for eſtabliſhing RELIGIOUS FREEDOM, *paſſed in the* ASSEMBLY *of* VIRGINNIA, *in the beginning of the Year,* 1786.

" WELL aware, that Almighty God hath created the mind free: that all attempts to influence it by temporal puniſhments or burthens, or by civil incapacitations, tend only to beget habits of hypocriſy, and are a departure from the plan of the Holy Author of our religion, who being Lord of body and mind, yet choſe not to propagate it by coercions on either--that the impious preſumption of legiſlators and rulers, civil as well as eccleſiaſtical (who being themſelves but fallible and uninſpired men, have aſſumed dominion over the faith of others, ſetting up their own opinion and modes of thinking as alone true and infallible, and as ſuch endeavouring to impoſe them on others), hath eſtabliſhed and maintained falſe religions over the greateſt part of the world, and through all time,— That, to compel a man to furniſh contributions of money for the propagation of opinions which he diſbelieves, is ſinful and tyrannical,—That even the forcing a man to ſupport this or that teacher of his own religious perſuaſion, is depriving him of the comfortable liberty of giving his contributions to the particular paſtor, whoſe morals he would make his pattern, and whoſe powers he feels moſt perſuaſive to righteouſneſs; and withdrawing from the miniſtry, thoſe temporal rewards, which, proceeding from an approbation of their perſonal conduct, are an additional incitement to earneſt and unremitted labours for the inſtruction of mankind,—That our civil rights have no dependence on our religious opinions, more than on our opinions in phyſic or geometry,—That, therefore, the proſcribing any citizen as unworthy the public confidence, by laying upon him an incapacity of being called to offices of truſt and emolument, unleſs he profeſs or renounce this or that religious opinion, is depriving him injuriouſly of thoſe privileges and advantages to which in common with his fellow-citizens he has a natural right; and tends alſo to corrupt the principles of that very religion it is meant to encourage, by bribing with a monopoly of worldly honours and emoluments, thoſe who will externally conform to it,—That though indeed thoſe are criminal who do not withſtand ſuch temptations, yet neither are thoſe innocent who lay them in their way,—That to ſuffer the civil magiſtrate to intrude his powers into the field of opinion, and to reſtrain the profeſſion or propagation of principles on ſuppoſition of their ill tendency, is a dangerous fallacy; which, at once deſtroys all religious liberty; becauſe he, being of courſe judge of that tendency, will make his opinions the rule of judgment, and approve or condemn the ſentiments of others, only as they ſhall agree with, or differ from his own—That it is time enough for the rightful purpoſes of civil government, for its officers to interpoſe when principles break out in overt acts againſt peace and good order. And finally, that truth is great, and will prevail if left to herſelf; is the proper and ſufficient antagoniſt to error; and can have nothing to fear from the conflict, unleſs by human interpoſition, diſarmed of her natural weapons (free argument and debate) error ceaſing to be dangerous, when it is permitted freely to contradict them.

" Be it therefore enacted by the General Aſſembly, that no man ſhall be compelled to ſupport any religious worſhip, place, or miniſtry whatſoever; nor ſhall be forced, reſtrained, moleſted or burthened in his body or goods, nor ſhall otherwiſe ſuffer, on account of his religious opinions or belief. But that all men be free to profeſs, and by argument to maintain, their opinion in matters of religion; and that the ſame ſhall in no wiſe diminiſh, enlarge, or affect their civil capacities.

" And though we well know that this Aſſembly, elected by the people for the ordinary purpoſes of legiſlation only, have no power to reſtrain the acts of ſucceeding Aſſemblies, conſtituted with powers equal to our own; and that, therefore, to declare this act irrevocable, would be of no effect in law; yet we are free to declare, and do declare, that the rights hereby aſſerted, are natural rights of mankind; and that if any act ſhall be hereafter paſſed to repeal the preſent, or to narrow its operation, ſuch act will be an infringement of natural rights."

Thomas Jefferson's "Act for Establishing Religious Freedom" of 1786 became a model for many states to support a broad religious freedom. It served as a basis for the First Amendment to the federal Constitution.

The goddess of American liberty denies entry of any religious group into the halls of government in this drawing by 19th-century political cartoonist Thomas Nast. Massachusetts was the last state to officially separate church and government, when it repealed its establishment of the Congregational Church as late as 1833.

state's towns were no longer collecting taxes for religious congregations, and in 1819 the legislature repealed the statute allowing the remaining towns to do so. In this regard, then, the failure of Connecticut and Massachsetts to repeal their establishment of the Congregational Church until 1818 and 1833 remained exceptions to the larger post-Revolutionary trend in religion to reject government aid and involvement.

The Virginia debate also affected the First Amendment to the federal Constitution, passed in 1791. The First Amendment used only 16 words to outline the relationship between religion and the new federal government: "Congress shall make no law respecting an establishment of religion, nor prohibit the free exercise thereof." Their meaning has, understandably, raised much debate over the years. In fact, the amendment reflected the nature of colonial American religious development even as it proposed an unprecedented course for society and religion in the new nation.

The First Amendment prohibited "an establishment of religion," not just of churches, by the new federal government. Commentators have long described the First Amendment as being about "church and state." Thomas Jefferson did so himself when he described the First Amendment as creating a "wall of separation between church and state" in a letter to the Danbury Baptist Association of Connecticut in 1802. But the First Amendment banned government activity in religion generally, not just the establishment of a national church. In debating the First Amendment, Congress specifically rejected changes that would have limited the amendment to issues such as "religious doctrine," "articles of faith or modes of worship," or merely prohibiting aid to "one religious sect or society in preference to others."

The First Amendment thus meant what it said and said what it meant. The federal government should not legislate on religious matters and should leave individuals alone in their pursuit of religion and religious truth. As Congressman Samuel Livermore of New York summarized the intentions of those who approved it, "Congress shall make no laws touching religion, or infringing the rights of conscience."

The First Amendment caught the essence of colonial America's religious development. It recognized the extraordinary, almost unimaginable diversity of religion that emerged in colonial America, a spiritual pluralism unlike that found in any society on either side of the Atlantic or Pacific. It guaranteed that government would not itself seek to change this diversity by intervening in religion or by supporting one or more religious groups. And it guaranteed that the federal government would uphold "free exercise" of religion for all groups, not just some.

No other government in Western civilization had ever before made such pledges. These pledges, together with the history of religion in the American colonies and the growth of religious diversity and activity in the next centuries, determined not only the health of religion in the United States but much about the character of its people.

Chronology

1607
Virginia settled

1620
The Pilgrims, radical Puritan separatists who had earlier fled to the Netherlands, land at Plymouth in Massachusetts

1624
The Church of England established in Virginia

1630
The main body of Puritans, led by John Winthrop, lands in Massachusetts

1634
Catholics settle Maryland under George Calvert

1636
Anne Hutchinson tried in Boston for sedition

1649
Laws upholding limited religious toleration passed in Maryland

1654
First Jews land in New Netherlands

1662
New England Congregationalists pass the "Half-Way Covenant"

1672–73
Quaker leader George Fox tours North Carolina, Virginia, and Maryland

1675–76
King Philip's War in New England destroys many "praying towns" of Indians converted to Christianity by John Eliot

1677
Puritan dissident John Rogers forms the sect called Rogerenes in Connecticut and Rhode Island

1682
Quakers settle Pennsylvania

1685
Philadelphia Yearly Meeting of Friends (Quakers) set up

French Protestant (Huguenot) refugees arrive in America after Louis XIV revokes the Edict of Nantes, which had protected Protestant worship since 1598

1692
Salem witch trials held

1692–93
Split occurs among Pennsylvania Quakers led by dissident George Keith

1694
African Burial Ground consecrated in New York City (closed in 1794)

1695
Church of England sets up first congregation in Puritan Boston

1700
Robert Calef of Boston publishes *More Wonders of the Invisible World,* denouncing Salem witch trials

1701

Church of England's Society for the Propagation of the Gospel in Foreign Parts (SPG) founded in London

1706

Presbytery of Philadelphia organized

1707

Philadelphia Baptist Association set up

1714

Massachusetts assembly reverses the verdicts of the Salem witch trials

1716

Synod of Philadelphia organized

1720

Theodorus Frelinghuysen begins to hold revivals among Dutch Reformed congregations in New Jersey

1730

The Amish begin settling in Pennsylvania

1728

Shearith Israel, New York City's first Jewish congregation purchases land for a cemetery and its first synagogue building

1739

George Whitefield arrives in the colonies to begin the first of seven preaching tours of the mainland colonies

1740

Gilbert Tennent publishes *The Danger of an Unconverted Ministry,* a pro-revivalist tract

1741

Jonathan Edwards first preaches his influential sermon "Sinners in the Hands of an Angry God" in Enfield, Massachusetts

Count Nicholas Zinzendorf and the Moravians arrive in the American colonies

1743

In Germantown, Pennsylvania, Christopher Sauer prints the first complete Bible in the British colonies, Martin Luther's version of the Bible

The revivalist James Davenport burns books and luxury goods in New London, Connecticut

1745

Pro-revivalist Presbyterian ministers form the Synod of New York and leave the old Synod of Philadelphia

1747

German Reformed Coetus, or assembly of ministers, is organized

1748

Lutheran Ministerium of Pennsylvania is set up

1756

Quakers begin reformation within their movement and withdraw from Pennsylvania politics

1758

Jonathan Edwards dies after receiving smallpox vaccination

Pro-revivalist and anti-revivalist Presbyterians reunite

1761

Rumors swirl about an alleged Anglican plot to install a bishop in the American colonies

1763

Touro Synagogue in Newport, Rhode Island, is dedicated

1764

Joanna Anthony successfully protests attempt to end female voting in Philadelphia's Baptist Church

1766–67

Sarah Osborn leads religious revivals in Newport, Rhode Island

1769

First Methodist preachers arrive in American colonies

1770

George Whitefield dies in Newburyport, Massachusetts

1774

British Parliament passes Quebec Act, which recognizes Catholicism as the religion of newly conquered French territory in Canada

1776

John Wesley withdraws Methodist preachers from the colonies in support of the Crown during the Revolution

1777

George Liele forms First African Church of Savannah, Georgia, a Baptist congregation

1779

Thomas Jefferson offers his "Bill for Establishing Religious Freedom" in Virginia

1786

Defeat of Patrick Henry's bill for a "multiple establishment" of religion in Virginia

Jefferson's "Bill for Establishing Religious Freedom" passed by Virginia's House of Burgesses

1787

Richard Allen and Absalom Jones form Free African Society in Philadelphia, progenitor of African Methodist Episcopal Church

1790

John Carroll of Maryland becomes first Roman Catholic bishop in the United States

1791

Ratification of First Amendment, saying in part, "Congress shall make no law respecting an establishment of religion, nor prohibit the free exercise thereof"

1797

Absalom Jones ordained first African-American Episcopal priest

Glossary

Amish A Mennonite dissident group led by Jacob Amman that arrived in Pennsylvania in the 1730s and 1740s and demanded greater separation from secular society.

Anglicans Members of the Church of England.

Ashkenazim Name given to European Jews who follow the rituals traditional to Jews in eastern and northern Europe.

Baptists Protestants who believe in the baptism of consenting adults rather than children. Most colonial Baptists were Calvinists who came from England and Wales, but some German Baptists ("Dunkers") also settled in the colonies in the eighteenth century.

Calvinists Followers of the theology of Genevan reformer John Calvin, who stressed God's omnipotence and salvation by God's grace alone.

Church of England The church established by Henry VIII at the time of the Protestant reformation. It rejected the authority of the pope and supported modest reforms in Catholic theology and liturgy but kept other features of Catholic worship and rejected more radical Protestant demands for change.

Congregationalists Protestants, usually Calvinists, who believe that each congregation should be self-governing and deny the authority of bishops, synods, or presbyteries. The Congregational movement grew out of the Puritan movement in England after the 1620s.

Diaspora The dispersion of a people or religious group, as in the scattering of Jews throughout Europe and North and South America after their expulsion from Spain and Portugal in 1492, or in the forced emigration of Africans to the Americas under the slave trade.

Dunkers Members of the German Baptist Brethren who emigrated to Pennsylvania from Germany in the 18th century. The term *Dunker* came from the German Brethren practice of baptizing believers by dunking them in a river or lake.

Evangelicalism A belief in the necessity of a personal "born again" religious experience, usually accompanied by an effort to reform one's personal life and to spread this religious enthusiasm to others.

Great Awakening Name given by 19th-century historians to religious revivals in England's American colonies between 1740 and 1770.

Lutherans Followers of the German reformer and originator of the Protestant reformation Martin Luther, who preached the doctrine of justification by faith alone rather than by good works and deeds.

Marranos The Spanish term applied to Jews forcibly converted to Christianity after the expulsion of the Jews from Spain in 1492.

Mennonites Followers of the 16th-century Frisian reformer Menno Simons, whose adherents practiced pacifism and emigrated to Pennsylvania in the 18th century.

Methodists Followers of the mid-18th-century Church of England reformers John and Charles Wesley.

The Wesleys preached Arminian doctrines that stressed the ability of individuals to achieve salvation by moral effort and spiritual renewal. Methodist leaders supported the Crown during the Revolutionary War but returned to America after the war and won many converts.

Moravians German Protestants who belonged to the Unitas Fratrum or Renewed Church of the United Brethren led by Count Nicholas Zinzendorf, who emigrated to Pennsylvania in 1741 and believed in the unification of all Protestants.

Occultism Belief in supernatural powers and in the secret knowledge inherent in these powers carried by special practitioners. Occult practices included alchemy (the attempt to transform base metals into gold), astrology (trying to calculate future actions based on the locations of the stars and planets), and witchcraft.

Pacifism Opposition to war and the use of violence in settling disputes; practiced by Quakers, Mennonites, and Moravians.

Pietism A movement originating in Lutheran Germany in the late 17th century that emphasized personal religious renewal and reform. The basis of many Protestant revival movements in the 18th century.

Presbyterians Protestants of the Calvinist persuasion who accept a hierarchical system of church government in which congregations submit to the authority of presbyteries and synods. The Presbyterian Church originated in Scotland under John Knox in the late 16th century.

Presbytery A meeting of ministers and selected laymen who exercise authority over congregations in a geographical district.

Protestant Episcopal Church The church formed after the American Revolution composed of congregations from the old Church of England.

Puritans English Calvinists who sought additional doctrinal and liturgical reform in the Church of England and settled the Massachusetts Bay Colony in 1630 under John Winthrop.

Quakers The popular and originally pejorative name given to members of the Society of Friends founded in England by George Fox in the 1650s. The Quakers believed in an "inward light" possessed by every individual and practiced pacifism.

Reformed Church The church in Germany that supported the Calvinist reformation.

Revivals Movements for religious renewal and reform often associated in the 18th century with emotional outbursts and rooted in a wide range of theologies from pietism to Calvinism.

Rogerenes A small offshoot of the New England Puritans led by John Rogers that was formed in the 1670s and became concentrated in eastern Connecticut and Rhode Island.

Roman Catholics Members of the Christian Church that traces its origins to the formation of Christianity, accepts the authority of the bishop of Rome (popularly known as the pope) as head of the church, and whose spiritual life centers on the seven sacraments of baptism, confirmation, holy eucharist, penance, anointing of the sick, holy orders, and matrimony.

Sect A religious group distinguished by its separation from society and its demand to conduct all business within the group, especially including marriage.

Separatists Radical Puritans who left England for the Netherlands in the 1610s to settle there, then emigrated to America in 1620, where they formed the Plymouth Bay Colony.

Sephardim Name given to European Jews who followed the traditional rituals common to Jews from Portugal and Spain.

Seven Sacraments The rites at the core of a Catholic life: baptism, confirmation, holy eucharist, penance, anointing of the sick, holy orders, and matrimony.

Shaman A religious figure, either male or female, common among many Native American religious groups who is said to possess special knowledge about the supernatural and nature, sometimes acts as a healer, and can perform both evil and good magic.

Suffragan A bishop with administrative responsibilities who cannot convene ecclesiastical courts.

Synod An assembly of ministers and selected laymen who exercise authority over both congregations and constituent presbyteries in a geographical district. The highest body in the Presbyterian system of church government.

Talmud The collected ancient rabbinic writings, consisting of the Mishna and the Gemara, that constitute the foundation of religious authority in Judaism.

Torah The first five books of the Hebrew Scriptures. A parchment scroll containing the text of the Torah is used in synagogue services.

Witchcraft Belief in the destructive powers of men or women who are said to have made compacts with the Devil that allow them to harm others or whose occult or secret knowledge is used for evil purposes.

Further Reading

GENERAL READING ON RELIGION IN THE UNITED STATES

Ahlstrom, Sidney. *A Religious History of the American People.* New Haven: Yale University Press, 1972.

Butler, Jon, and Harry S. Stout, eds. *Religion in American History: A Reader.* New York: Oxford University Press, 1997.

Gaustad, Edwin. *A Religious History of America.* Rev. ed. San Francisco: Harper & Row, 1990.

Marty, Martin. *Pilgrims in Their Own Land: 500 Years of Religion in America.* New York: Penguin, 1985.

WORLDS OLD AND NEW

Bossy, John. *Christianity in the West, 1400–1700.* New York: Oxford University Press, 1985.

Butler, Jon. *Awash in a Sea of Faith: Christianizing the American People.* Cambridge, Mass.: Harvard University Press, 1990.

Crawford, Patricia. *Women and Religion in England, 1500–1750.* New York: Routledge, 1996.

Ginzburg, Carlo. *The Cheese and the Worms: The Cosmos of a Sixteenth-Century Miller.* Trans. John and Anne Tedeschi. Baltimore, Md.: Johns Hopkins University Press, 1992.

Ozment, Steven E. *Protestants: The Birth of a Revolution.* New York: Doubleday, 1992.

Thomas, Keith. *Religion and the Decline of Magic.* New York: Charles Scribner's Sons, 1971.

Thornton, John. *Africa and Africans in the Making of the Atlantic World, 1400–1680.* New York: Cambridge University Press, 1992.

RELIGION IN THE FIRST COLONIES

Brydon, G. MacLaren. *Virginia's Mother Church and the Political Conditions Under Which It Grew.* 2 vols. Philadelphia: Church Historical Society, 1947.

Demos, John Putnam. *Entertaining Satan: Witchcraft and the Culture of Early New England.* New York: Oxford University Press, 1982.

Ellis, John Tracy. *Catholics in Colonial America.* Baltimore, Md.: Helicon, 1965.

———. *Worlds of Wonder, Days of Judgment: Popular Religious Belief in Early New England.* New York: Knopf, 1989.

Miller, Perry. *Errand into the Wilderness.* Cambridge, Mass.: Harvard University Press, 1956.

Morgan, Edmund S. *The Puritan Dilemma: The Story of John Winthrop.* Boston: Little, Brown, 1958.

Rightmyer, Nelson W. *Maryland's Established Church.* Baltimore: Church Historical Society for the Diocese of Maryland, 1956.

Rutman, Darrett B. *Winthrop's Boston: Portrait of a Puritan Town, 1630–1649.* Chapel Hill: University of North Carolina Press, 1965.

Stout, Harry S. *The New England Soul: Preaching and Religious Culture in Colonial New England.* New York: Oxford University Press, 1986.

Ziff, Larzer. *The Career of John Cotton: Puritanism and the American Experience.* Princeton, N.J.: Princeton University Press, 1962.

THE FLOWERING OF RELIGIOUS DIVERSITY

Balmer, Randall H. *A Perfect Babel of Confusion: Dutch Religion and English Culture in the Middle Colonies.* New York: Oxford University Press, 1989.

Butler, Jon. *The Huguenots in America: A Refugee People in New World Society.* Cambridge, Mass.: Harvard University Press, 1983.

Dunn, Mary Maples. *William Penn: Politics and Conscience.* Princeton, N.J.: Princeton University Press, 1967.

Faber, Eli. *A Time for Planting: The First Migration, 1654–1820.* Baltimore, Md.: Johns Hopkins University Press, 1992.

Gollin, Gillian Lindt. *Moravians in Two Worlds: A Study of Changing Communities.* New York: Columbia University Press, 1967.

Landsman, Ned. *Scotland and Its First American Colony, 1683–1765.* Princeton, N.J.: Princeton University Press, 1985.

Levy, Barry. *Quakers and the American Family: British Settlement in the Delaware Valley.* New York: Oxford University Press, 1988.

Richey, Russell E. *Early American Methodism.* Bloomington: Indiana University Press, 1991.

Roeber, A. G. *Palatines, Liberty and Property: German Lutherans in British North America.* Baltimore, Md.: Johns Hopkins University Press, 1993.

Tolles, Frederick B. *Meeting House and Counting House: The Quaker Merchants of Colonial Philadelphia, 1682–1763.* Chapel Hill: University of North Carolina Press, 1948.

Walters, Kerry S. *Benjamin Franklin and His Gods.* Urbana: University of Illinois Press, 1999.

Woolverton, John F. *Colonial Anglicanism in North America.* Detroit: Wayne State University Press, 1984.

AFRICAN AND AMERICAN INDIAN RELIGION

Frey, Sylvia R., and Betty Wood. *Come Shouting to Zion: African American Protestantism in the American South and British Caribbean to 1830.* Chapel Hill: University of North Carolina Press, 1998.

Martin, Joel W. *Sacred Revolt: The Muskogees' Struggle for a New World.* Boston: Beacon, 1991.

Merrell, James H. *The Indians' New World: Catawbas and Their Neighbors from European Contact Through the Era of Removal.* Chapel Hill: University of North Carolina Press,1989.

Raboteau, Albert J. *Slave Religion: The "Invisible Institution" in the Antebellum South.* New York: Oxford University Press, 1978.

Sensbach, Jon F. *A Separate Canaan: The Making of an Afro-Moravian World in North Carolina, 1763–1840.* Chapel Hill: University of North Carolina Press, 1997.

Sobel, Mechal. *Trabelin' On: The Slave Journey to an Afro-Baptist Faith.* Westport, Conn.: Greenwood, 1979.

REVIVING COLONIAL RELIGION

Bonomi, Patricia U. *Under the Cope of Heaven: Religion, Society, and Politics in Colonial America.* New York: Oxford University Press, 1986.

Brekus, Catherine A. *Strangers and Pilgrims: Female Preaching in America, 1740–1845.* Chapel Hill: University of North Carolina Press, 1998.

Gaustad, Edwin S. *The Great Awakening in New England.* New York: Harper & Row, 1957.

Juster, Susan. *Disorderly Women: Sexual Politics and Evangelicalism in Revolutionary New England.* Ithaca, N.Y.: Cornell University Press, 1994.

Schmidt, Leigh Eric. *Holy Fairs: Scottish Communions and American Revivals in the Early Modern Period.* Princeton, N.J.: Princeton University Press, 1989.

Stout, Harry S. *The Divine Dramatist: George Whitefield and the Rise of Modern Evangelicalism.* Grand Rapids, Mich.: Eerdmans, 1991.

Tracy, Patricia J. *Jonathan Edwards, Pastor: Religion and Society in Eighteenth Century Northampton.* New York: Hill and Wang, 1980.

Upton, Del. *Holy Things and Profane: Anglican Parish Churches in Colonial Virginia.* Cambridge, Mass.: MIT Press, 1986.

RELIGION AND THE AMERICAN REVOLUTION

Albanese, Catherine L. *Sons of the Fathers: The Civil Religion of the American Revolution.* Philadelphia: Temple University Press, 1976.

Bloch, Ruth H. *Visionary Republic: Millennial Themes in American Thought, 1756–1800.* New York: Cambridge University Press, 1985.

Frey, Sylvia R. *Water from the Rock: Black Resistance in a Revolutionary Age.* Princeton, N.J.: Princeton University Press, 1991.

Gaustad, Edwin Scott. *Faith of Our Fathers: Religion and the New Nation.* San Francisco: Harper & Row, 1987.

Marini, Stephen A. *Radical Sects of Revolutionary New England.* Cambridge, Mass.: Harvard University Press, 1982.

Noll, Mark A. *Christians in the American Revolution.* Washington, D.C: Christian University Press, 1977.

Rhoden, Nancy L. *Revolutionary Anglicanism: The Colonial Church of England Clergy During the American Revolution.* New York: New York University Press, 1999.

Sarna, Jonathan, Benny Kraut, and Samuel K. Joseph. *Jews and the Founding of the Republic.* New York: Markus Wiener, 1985.

Index

Picture Credits

Abby Aldrich Rockefeller Folk Art Center, Williamsburg, VA: 90; Courtesy, American Antiquarian Society: 2, 32, 45, 108; American Jewish Historical Society, Waltham, MA and New York, NY: 63; Photograph reprinted by permission of the American Tract Society, Garland, TX: 99; Archive Photos: 58, 64, 83, 124; Art Resource: 13, 20, 27, 135; Ashmolean Museum, Oxford: 28; © Copyright The British Museum: 85, 123; Champlain Society: 81; Department of Special Collections, Charles E. Young Research Library, UCLA: 72, 115; Colonial Williamsburg Foundation: 120, 137; Congregation Mikveh Israel: 106; The Connecticut Historical Society, Hartford, CT: 112; Delaware Art Museum: 74; By Permission of the Folger Shakespeare Library: 48; Copyright Gibbes Museum of Art / Carolina Art Association: 55; Burlington Hexagonal Friends Meeting House, Courtesy the Quaker Collection, Haverford College Library: 68; © John T. Hopf: 61; Courtesy of the John Carter Brown Library at Brown University: 125; John Street United Methodist Church: cover; Fulham Papers, Lambeth Palace Library: 14; Library of Congress: 10, 17, 23, 30, 35, 43, 49, 67, 80, 105, 132, 139 (Broadside Collection, Rare Book and Special Collections Division),140; Lyman Allyn Museum of Art at Connecticut College, New London, CT: 96; Courtesy of the Massachusetts Historical Society: 92, 107; Courtesy, Museum of Fine Arts, Boston, reproduced with permission, © 1999 Museum of Fine Arts, Boston, all rights reserved: 118; Photo courtesy of The Newberry Library, Chicago: 51; New York Public Library: 34, 50, 104; Collection of Old Salem: 59; Courtesy Peabody Essex Museum, Salem, MA: 39; Pierpont Morgan Library: 79; Museum of Art, Rhode Island School of Design, gift of Lucy Truman Aldrich, photography by Erik Gould: 93; © Professor Robert Ferris Thompson: 25; "First Sudbury Meeting House," fig. 17 from *Puritan Village: The Formation of a New England Town* by Sumner Chilton Powell © 1963, Wesleyan University Press, reprinted by permission of University Press of New England: 102; Werner Forman Archive/Art Resource: 26, 77; Yale University: 6 (Harold Wickliffe Rose Collection), 111 (Art Gallery, Bequest of Eugene Phelps Edwards), 126 (Courtesy of the Print Collection, Lewis Walpole Library); The Historical Society of York County, PA, Lewis Miller (1796–1882): 52, 57; Zeist, Evangelische Broedergemeente: 89.

Text Credits

"A Puritan Leader Speaks to Early American Emigrants," p. 33: *The Winthrop Papers* (Boston: Massachusetts Historical Society, 1931), vol. 2.

"A Mother Laments Her Daughter's Faithlessness," pp. 62–63: Leo Hershkowitz and Isidor S. Meyer, eds., *Letters of the Franks Family (1733–1748)* (Waltham, Mass.: American Jewish Historical Society, 1968).

"A Christian Missionary Learns about Native Americans' Religion," pp. 86–87: David Brainerd, *Mirabilia Dei inter Indicos; or, The Rise and Progress of a Remarkable Work of Grace Amongst a Number of the Indians in the Provinces of New Jersey and Pennsylvania, Justly Represented in a Journal Kept by Order of the Honourable Society (in Scotland) for Propagating Christian Knowledge* (Edinburgh, 1765).

"Jonathan Edwards Rouses a Congregation," p. 111: John E. Smith, Harry S. Stout, and Kenneth P. Minkema, *A Jonathan Edwards Reader* (New Haven: Yale University Press, 1995).

"Sarah Osborn Leads African-American Religious Revivals," pp. 116–17: Mary Beth Norton, "'My Resting Reaping Times': Sarah Osborn's Defense of Her 'Unfeminine Activities,'" *Signs* 2 (1976).

"Presbyterian Caution about the American Revolution," pp. 128–29: *Records of the Presbyterian Church in the United States of America, 1706–1788* (Philadelphia: Presbyterian Board of Publication and Sabbath-School Work, 1904).

Jon Butler

Jon Butler is the William Robertson Coe Professor of American Studies and History and Professor of Religious Studies at Yale University. He received his B.A. and Ph.D. in history from the University of Minnesota. He is the coauthor, with Harry S. Stout, of *Religion in American History: A Reader*, and the author of several other books in American religious history including *Awash in a Sea of Faith: Christianizing the American People*, which won the Beveridge Award for the best book in American history in 1990 from the American Historical Association.

Harry S. Stout

Harry S. Stout is the Jonathan Edwards Professor of American Christianity at Yale University. He is the general editor of the Religion in America series for Oxford University Press and co-editor of *Readings in American Religious History, New Directions in American Religious History, A Jonathan Edwards Reader*, and *The Dictionary of Christianity in America*. His book *The Divine Dramatist: George Whitefield and the Rise of Modern Evangelicalism* was nominated for a Pulitzer Prize in 1991.